Words of Our Mouth, Meditations of Our Heart

WORDS OF OUR MOUTH, MEDITATIONS OF OUR HEART

Pioneering Musicians of Ska, Rocksteady, Reggae, and Dancehall

Kenneth Bilby

WESLEYAN UNIVERSITY PRESS | MIDDLETOWN, CONNECTICUT

Wesleyan University Press
Middletown CT 06459
www.wesleyan.edu/wespress

Manufactured in the United States of America
Designed by April Leidig
Typeset in Kepler by Copperline Book Services, Inc.

Frontispiece: Buru drumming across the generations.
Old Harbour Bay, Jamaica, 2005.

Library of Congress Cataloging-in-Publication Data
Bilby, Kenneth M., 1953–
Words of our mouth, meditations of our heart:
pioneering musicians of ska, rocksteady, reggae,
and dancehall / Kenneth Bilby.
pages cm.—(Music/interview)
Includes index.
ISBN 978-0-8195-7588-3 (pbk. : alk. paper)
ISBN 978-0-8195-7604-0 (ebook)
1. Musicians—Jamaica—Interviews. 2. Popular music—
Jamaica—History and criticism. I. Title.
ML3486.J3B45 2016
781.646097292—dc23 2015022537

5 4 3 2 1

Contents

Words and Images

Give Thanks

The larger research project that provided the materials for this book has been many years in the making, and has benefited from the goodwill and kind gestures of many, including some who offered help of one kind or another long before the book itself was even imagined. Reaching back across the years, I hope my memory is up to the task of gathering together and recognizing here all those who have played some part.

For inspirational early conversations and interviews (years before this project was conceived), I thank Horace Andy, Jimmy Cliff, Donald Davidson (of the Jolly Boys), the late Desmond Dekker, Lord Laro, Lloyd Lovindeer, the late Junior Murvin, Ras Michael, Winston Rodney (Burning Spear), the late David Scott (Scotty), and the late Peter Tosh.

For essential help with tracking down and contacting particular musicians (once this project was in motion), I thank Dennis Alcapone, Wayne Armond, Andy Bassford, Virgil Bland, Bunny Brown, Glen Browne, Andrea Bullens, Charles Cameron, Frankie Campbell and JAVAA (Jamaica Association of Vintage Artists and Affiliates), Claudelle Clarke, Brother Sam Clayton, Tony Clayton, Gary Crosby, Jim Dooley, Luke Ehrlich (The White Ram), Steve Golding, the late Winston Grennan, Joe Hilton, Jake Homiak, Joe Isaacs, Ruddy Isaacs, Jackie Jackson, Tony Johnson (Jamaka, aka Tee Birdd), Desi Jones, Al Kaatz, Brian Keyo, Elliott Leib, Colin Leslie, Charmaine Limonius, John Masouri, Larry McDonald, Clive McKerney (Jah Roots), Vin Morgan, Dan Neely, Ken Parker, Dave Rosencrans, Cheryl Ryman, the late Robert Schoenfeld, Roger Steffens, Carter Van Pelt, Marjorie Whylie, and Mark Williams.

Special thanks go to the phenomenal Herbie Miller, who knows just about everybody in the world of Jamaican popular music, and who generously opened his address book and helped open innumerable doors for me in Kingston and beyond.

For moral support, good words, and good deeds, I thank David Aarons, Roger Abrahams, the late Gerard Béhague, Bryan Bilby, John Chernoff, John Cowley, Elizabeth Branch Dyson, DJ Emch, Bill Ferris, Samuel Floyd, Ray Funk, Don Hill, Richard Price, Wynne Racine, the late Johns Storm Roberts, Roswell Rudd, Cheryl Ryman, Nini Salet, Guha Shankar, Margot Snellback, and Jason Toynbee.

For invaluable critical feedback on early drafts of the book, I thank Garnette Cadogan, Jefferson Miller, and Wynne Racine.

For illuminating discussions, special insights, and groundbreaking cultural work, I thank Dennis Bovell, the late Cedric Brooks, Linton Kwesi Johnson, the late Rex Nettleford, and Garth White.

For material and logistical support, I thank the John Simon Guggenheim Memorial Foundation, the Rockefeller Foundation, and the Center for Black Music Research in Chicago.

For many years of valued correspondence and inspiring poetry, and for making sure that this book saw the light of day, I thank Norm Weinstein.

For their friendship and for additional help in ways impossible to label, I thank my Big Bredda Charles Cameron (Charley Organaire) and my Likkle Bredda Garnette Cadogan.

For their loving care, and for helping to make both music and Jamaica so much a part of my life, I thank my mother, Helen Owen Bilby, and my grandmother, Kitty Owen.

Along with thanks, I must offer apologies to the several musicians and singers who contributed interviews to my project but could not be included in this book mainly because I lacked suitable photographs—among them such well-known figures as Toots Hibbert (of the Maytals), Family Man Barrett (of the Wailers), and the late Lloyd Knibb (of the Skatalites), as well as a number of lesser known but no less important contributors, such as Ranford "Ronnie Bop" Williams (pioneering session guitarist), Earl "Bagga" Walker (prolific session bassist), and Tony King (original session percussionist). Though their literal words and images are absent, their presence can still be felt in this book.

Other important musicians I would have particularly liked to include, such as session drummer Lloyd "Tinleg" Adams, session bassist Brian Atkinson, and session guitarist Earl "Chinna" Smith, are not here because I ran out of time and resources before I could get to them; yet others, such as keyboardist Jackie Mittoo, saxophonists Roland Alphonso and Tommy McCook, and percussionist Denzil Laing, were no longer alive when I started the project. Among those I barely missed, hearing of their passing just as I was hot on their trail, were drummer Hugh Malcolm and guitarist Eric "Rickenbacker" Frater. I will always regret not having had the opportunity to sit down and talk with these notable innovators.

There are so many more elders of Jamaican popular music I would have liked to meet and interview, many of them still living. But Jamaica has produced an amazing amount of musical talent, and the number of "vintage" singers and musicians deserving of attention is much too large for any one investigator to hope to tackle. And so I must add my thanks as well to those researchers and writers—many of them music journalists—who have done interviewing of their own, including Heather Augustyn, Steve Barrow, Bruno Blum, Lloyd Bradley, Howard Campbell, Laurence Cane-Honeysett, Mel Cooke, Stephen Davis, Jim Dooley, Thibault Ehrengardt, Chuck Foster, Carl Gayle, Vivien Goldman, Bunny Goodison, Mark Gorney, Colby Graham, Randall Grass, Noel Hawks, Dave Hendley, Balford Henry, Ray Hitchins, Aad van der Hoek, Hank Holmes, Dennis Howard, Ray Hurford, Dermot Hussey, Clinton Hutton, Peter I, Tim Ianna, Brian Jahn, the late Tero Kaski, David Katz, Rob Kenner, Brian Keyo, Jérémie Kroubo Dagnini, Michael Kuelker, Chris Lane, Hélène Lee, Beth Lesser, Rich Lowe, John Masouri, Chris May, Daniel Neely, M. Peggy Quattro, Penny Reel, Amon Saba Saakana, the late Robert Schoenfeld, Mick Sleeper, Roger Steffens, Norman Stolzoff, Angus Taylor, Carter Van Pelt, Michael Veal, Pekka Vuorinen, Klive Walker, Tom Weber, Doug Wendt, the late Timothy White, Chris Wilson, and a handful of others. They have helped to preserve an important part of the history of Jamaican popular music, and I am grateful for the body of work they have published, which has provided me with a useful base for cross-checking and comparison.

Thanks are due as well to my editors at Wesleyan University Press, especially Parker Smathers and Elizabeth Forsaith, for their steadfast support and the improvements they brought to what you see in the following pages. I am grateful also to designer April Leidig for helping to make the book so pleasing to the eye.

Above all, I give thanks to the originators of Jamaican music who appear in this book. Their music has given me untold pleasure and inspiration over the years, and I continue to marvel at their accomplishments. Sitting down and sharing thoughts with them was a rare privilege, and even more rewarding than I imagined it would be.

Introduction

Let the words of our mouth,
And the meditation of our heart,
Be acceptable in thy sight,
O Far I
—Devotional lyric adapted by
Jamaican worshipers from Psalm 19

"The half has never been told." This oft-repeated phrase holds the key to a fundamental Jamaican truth, reminding each generation that no matter how much we think we know, there is always more—much more—to the story. Only with time, patience, and determination can what has long remained hidden be revealed. Nothing in Jamaica embodies this truth better than its music.

The voices and faces in this book speak to this truth from a special vantage point. Not only were these pioneers present when the earliest styles of Jamaican popular music were being born; more important, they themselves were some of the first *players* and shapers of these styles. Without their creative work, this music, as we know it, quite simply would not exist. Without their portion of the half that remains untold—their memories of the early days and the unique perspectives they can bring—there can be little hope of arriving at a balanced understanding of this music and how it came to be. Their truth is at the heart of this book.

Once scorned and neglected in both its homeland and the Euro-American Capitals of Culture, Jamaica's popular music has gone on to capture the hearts and minds of people everywhere—and I do mean *everywhere*. While it is clear enough that this music (and here we must include the distinct genres of ska, rocksteady, and dancehall/ragga along with reggae) has risen to the status of a global art form over the last few decades, it is probably safe to say that no one knows just how vast its actual reach is today. It would take an army of researchers with unlimited time and resources to tally all the local permutations Jamaican music has left in its wake while penetrating virtually every corner of our planet. What we do know is that reggae, like its American cousin hip-hop, has crossed virtually every conceivable border and become one of the world's most prominent sounds. How could one of the smallest and most economically challenged countries on earth produce a music of such astonishing boundary-breaching power? This in itself remains an enigma—a part, perhaps, of the "half that has never been told."

Given its remarkable leap from obscurity and disdain to worldwide influence, it is hard to avoid the sense that there is something special and inexplicable about Jamaica's popular music. What are the actual cultural wellsprings of this music, and who exactly are its creators? Despite the millions of words exchanged about the mysteries of Jamaican music since the global rise of reggae, the readily available answers, in my view, are far from satisfactory. This book is fueled partly by my frustration at this lack of adequate answers to basic questions.

THE NEW SOUNDS of ska, rocksteady, reggae, and dancehall—the distinctive genres of popular music that the world now identifies as Jamaican—came into being primarily in the recording studios of Kingston. On this point there seems to be general agreement. Although the dawn of Jamaica's recording industry can actually be traced back to the early 1950s, when a handful of cottage enterprises emerged to produce records in the homegrown mento style for limited markets, it was not until the early 1960s that an explosion of recording activity began, unleashing an extraordinary new wave of musical creativity. The birth of Jamaica's first urban popular music, ska, coincided precisely with the sudden appearance of full-fledged, modern recording facilities in the capital of the newly independent nation, and the major stylistic shifts that followed, from rocksteady through reggae and dub, grew directly out of Kingston's rapidly evolving studio culture.

The existence of studios depended on certain things. A basic infrastructure was required, including a physical building, recording equipment, and musical instruments. Technicians were needed, including studio designers, recording engineers, and trained maintenance personnel. Some form of centralized economic management was indispensable, as were individual "producers" who possessed (or were able to scrape together) the financial means to initiate and enable recording sessions. None of this would have amounted to anything, however, without proficient *musicians*—individuals capable of making appealing musical sounds that could be captured on tape and then rendered into marketable products. In a very real sense, these musicians were the most important link in the chain, the foundation upon which everything else stood. *They* were the primary creators, the producers of first instance. Their livings depended on their ability to come up with novel sounds in the studio that people would want to listen to, dance to, and buy. Because of the demands placed on them, they were the primary architects of new and original musical styles.

This elementary point, you would think, should be self-evident. Yet it has gone largely unrecognized in the voluminous literature on Jamaican popular music. In fact, the fundamental contribution made by these studio musicians remains woefully underacknowledged. This omission can be attributed in part to certain peculiarities that became entrenched early on as the recording of Jamaican music developed into a profitable business. The bosses in this new enterprise were the studio owners and the producers who assembled musicians for sessions and paid for studio time. Session musicians most often were hired on an ad hoc basis, being paid per song or individual recording. Their creative labor was treated as a kind of piecework, the end product of which belonged solely to those who had paid for it. Not only did producers own and control the resulting master tapes, which they were free to convert into marketable commodities as they wished, but they often felt that they owned the music itself in perpetuity. Some even went so far as to claim authorship (or coauthorship), crediting themselves on record labels as composers, and in some cases copyrighting or publishing songs in their own names.

There were, in fact, many more pieces to this puzzle, and students of Jamaican music will be teasing out the complex factors involved in the growth of this somewhat chaotic local music industry for years to come. On the creative side of things, one can single out certain prominent contributors who played an important role alongside the instrumentalists who provided the musical bedrock. These include singers, songwriters, arrangers, and audio engineers. But as more information comes to light about the recording process during the critical formative years, it becomes increasingly apparent that a large majority of the creative work, especially during this early period, fell on the shoulders of the session musicians who ultimately were responsible for inventing the musical frameworks (and with the advent of multitrack recording, the backing tracks and fundamental "riddims") upon which hit records (and later, dub versions and deejay tracks) were constructed. More often than not, singers arrived in the studio with little more than a sketch of a song, consisting of partial lyrics and a tentative melody devoid of a harmonic progression or arrangement. The musicians routinely supplied the critical missing elements (including the song's rhythmic structure) on the spot, through a collaborative process of experimentation and playing-in-the-moment—what might be thought of as a kind of spontaneous composition. These session musicians, in effect, actually doubled as co-composers and arrangers.

Seldom did the producer in charge of a session contribute specific musical suggestions to this fast-moving creative process (although there were exceptions). Indeed, producers were often not even present at the actual sessions. For this reason,

Jamaica's foundational session musicians often point out the need to qualify the term "producer." It would be more accurate, they say, to characterize most of those who bore this title as "executive producers," meaning simply the parties who financed the production. According to these musicians, those who typically styled themselves "producers" in Jamaica (with rare exceptions, such as the legendary Lee "Scratch" Perry) were producers only in this financial sense and had very little to do with the actual creation of the music they ended up controlling. Creatively speaking, these musicians insist, they themselves were most often their own producers (although they sometimes also credit audio engineers for innovative contributions, which could feed back into the ways session musicians thought about and played their music).

The peculiar way in which the local recording industry was structured led to a perverse outcome. As markets for Jamaican music expanded over time and the economic potential of the music, including older recordings, increased exponentially, the actual creators of the music watched while the "producers"—those who held the master recordings (and sometimes the legal rights)—received most or all of the resulting windfall. Studio musicians were not alone in being deprived of what they saw as their just deserts. Singers (who often were also songwriters) shared this embittering experience, for most of their recordings had been made before the notion of copyright had gained any real traction in Jamaica. As they became aware that recordings featuring their voices (and sometimes songs they had written) were now being sold around the world for profits they would never see, they found that they had little or no legal recourse, since they lacked proper documentation of the circumstances of composition or recording. But the session musicians—the instrumentalists on whose talents the entire enterprise rested—suffered the added indignity of receiving virtually no credit for their efforts. While some singers at least achieved a measure of fame and were able to translate this into new opportunities for live performance and touring abroad, most of the foundational musicians, as times changed and new musical trends took over, were forgotten and languished in obscurity.

Adding insult to injury, many of the first generation of "producers" themselves went on to gain a certain celebrity, eclipsing the musicians who had worked for them. Confronted with a growing variety of Jamaican releases that typically featured prominent "production" credits but little or no information on instrumentalists, fans began to identify particular sonic qualities and stylistic traits with specific studios and producers rather than the revolving "stables" of musicians on whom they depended. "Producers" became as "legendary" for what was thought of as "their" music as for the romanticized stories told about their exploits in Jamaica's "cutthroat" music business. To a large extent, scholars, music journalists, and other writers have followed suit, treating well-known producers, most of whom were essentially small businessmen looking to turn a quick profit, as if they deserve primary credit for the creative output of the musicians they employed on a temporary basis. Strange as it might seem, the names (or nicknames) of these nonmusician entrepreneurs (for example, Clement "Sir Coxsone" Dodd, Arthur "Duke" Reid, Harry Johnson ["Harry J"], Bunny "Striker" Lee, Vincent "Randy" Chin, Joel Gibson ["Joe Gibbs"], Lloyd "Matador" Daley, Sonia Pottinger, Lawrence Lindo ["Jack Ruby"], Joseph ["Jo Jo"] Hookim, Alvin "G.G." Ranglin, and Leslie Kong, among others) are today much more likely to be recognized by aficionados of reggae than those of the founding musicians who actually created and performed the sounds that mean so much to so many around the world.

If one chooses to focus on the founding musicians themselves, rather than their employers, the implications are far-reaching. Consider the backgrounds of these foundational players. Although formally trained and highly experienced professional musicians always have played an important role in Jamaican studios—and during the transition from American-style rhythm and blues to ska they were particularly prominent—sessions were, from the beginning, open to anyone who could bring interesting musical ideas and could play with the right "feel." Over time, as migration from rural areas increased, more and more people from Kingston's expanding periphery, many of them recently arrived from country parts, turned to the rapidly growing music industry as a means of subsistence. Although few in Jamaica could afford a formal education in music, life across the island was full of music of a noncommoditized kind—music that formed part of the fabric of daily life—and some of those who had participated in such "traditional" musical settings in the countryside or on the urban fringe might well think of themselves as bearers of "natural" musical gifts. As it turned out, more than a few such individuals were able to work up the courage to try their hands in the studios, and before long they were to become a critical part of the mix that produced Jamaica's distinctive popular sound.

Whether urban or rural, trained or untrained, session musicians are key to the understanding of how this popular music evolved. As a vernacular tradition, a genuine "people's music," reggae (in its broadest sense) has always been viewed by the society from which it sprang as an expression of something greater than individual creativity (although individual artistry is certainly appreciated in Jamaica). Like all popular musics, its success, artistic as well as commercial, depended on broad appeal. As the business of Jamaican popular music grew, the participants in the best position to coax forth new sounds that would appeal to the broadest possible cross-section of the population were not those who happened to be skilled in the arts of promotion and marketing, but rather those who, at a profound level, shared a preexisting musical language with the majority of their countrymen and were capable, in the contrived setting of the studio, of translating this effectively into fresh and original, yet locally rooted, syntheses. Rather than the "producers" who provided them with material incentives, or the mobile sound systems that made their recordings available to the masses and became a crucial part of the feedback loop on which they depended, it was Jamaica's hard-working session musicians themselves who represented the primary creative interface between Jamaican popular music and the Jamaican people.

PERSONAL AS WELL AS professional predilections lie behind this book. Jamaican sounds have been with me from as far back as I can remember. My maternal grandmother lived a good portion of her life on the island. After growing up in Kingston as a young child in the early 1900s and then moving to the United States, she returned to spend much of her adult life in the northern parish of St. Ann between the 1940s and 1970s. She had a keen ear and an artist's eye, and Jamaica's physical beauty and cultural richness had much to do with her choice to take up residence there once again as an adult. My mother, in turn, absorbed Caribbean rhythmic and melodic sensibilities in her youth while visiting my grandmother in Jamaica, and also while participating as an amateur musician and composer in the North American vogue for calypso music during the 1940s and 1950s. One of my fondest early memories is that of romping on my hands and knees underneath my mother's baby grand piano to the magical outpouring of Caribbean-derived rhythms overhead.

My first trip to Jamaica occurred when I was too young to remember anything. But musical memories from later in my childhood have stayed with me. I can remember the strains of mento played by string bands at tourist spots in and around Kingston, the fifing and drumming of Jonkonnu troupes parading outdoors over the Christmas holidays, and the barely audible pulse of unseen drums wafting across the jasmine-laced night air of the St. Ann hills. At a tender age, I began to associate these sounds with the sensory wonders of the environment in which I encountered them—the amazingly lush landscape, the profusion of powerful fragrances, the vibrant colors, the narrow streets bustling with unfamiliar cadences of speech and movement, and the incredible brilliance of the Caribbean moon. While still a young child, I learned from concerned Jamaicans to be aware of duppies, or ghosts, which, I was told, inhabited the tangled roots of cotton trees but also wandered about at night and could become troublesome and dangerous if encountered under the wrong circumstances. I came to feel that the entire place was pervaded by spirits, especially at night, and all the music I heard in Jamaica as a child—even some of the more familiar American tunes coming out of radios—somehow came to be imbued with a peculiarly Jamaican spiritual charge. Though only a visitor, and though my contacts with Jamaicans were mostly superficial, it was hard at this impressionable age not to come under the spell of the island.

Later still, on visits to my grandmother as a young teenager, I remember being intrigued by the rumbling bass and pumping accents of rocksteady and early reggae while passing sound systems on the streets of St. Ann's Bay, scarcely aware that I was witnessing the birth of a major new form of music. I remember late one night, toward the end of the 1960s, happening upon a Jamaican band playing on a small stage for a local crowd of dancers at a rough-edged nightspot in Ocho Rios. As potent as the vaguely familiar beat was, I was too fixed on the countercultural energy of the rock explosion then dominating the U.S. airwaves to pay more than passing attention. I remember another time, at age sixteen, accompanying a group of friends on a trip into the hills of St. Ann to sample the wisdom of some dreadlocked Rastafarian brethren; the local music that was a conspicuous part of the backdrop made only a vague impression at the time. It wasn't that I was completely oblivious to the signs at every turn that some new cultural energy was bubbling up in Jamaica. But music had always been everywhere in Jamaica, and people seemed to take it for granted. I took it for granted too.

In the 1970s, when I entered college and began to study ethnomusicology, it seemed only natural for me to gravitate back to Jamaica. The island's first film of note, *The Harder They Come,* starring Jimmy Cliff, had recently become a cult hit in the United States, and Bob Marley's star was on the rise as well. Under Prime Minister Michael Manley, Jamaica had become a major force in progressive Third World politics, and the country's burgeoning popular music scene had much to do with its sudden entry onto the world stage. Having continued to visit my grandmother in Jamaica into the new decade, I had witnessed some of this from close up. Yet, as inspiring as these new trends in music and politics were, I was drawn at first not to the rapidly shifting soundscape of urban Jamaica but to the older musical traditions of the countryside that resonated with memories from my childhood.

So, unlike most foreigners discovering Jamaica's music, I focused at first on the "traditional" (the "roots"), leaving the "popular" (the "branches") for later. Even then, I realized that the conventional partitioning of these imagined domains into separate worlds was not to be given too much credence in the Jamaican context.

While working in rural Jamaica as a budding ethnomusicologist and participating as often as possible in traditional musical events, I also spent a fair amount of time in record shops sampling the latest reggae tunes and went to my share of booming all-night sound system dances for the pure pleasure of it. These popular musical sites were among the hot spots of an emerging youth-oriented "roots" culture for which a newfound Rastafari consciousness was the main catalyst. One of the fruits of this youth culture was the newly ascendant genre that later was to become known to the world outside Jamaica as "roots reggae." In those days, young "knotty dreads" in the cultural vanguard would greet one another on the streets of the city with the slogan, "Roots!" The entire society seemed to be turning "forward," as Rastas would say, through a redemptive appeal to Jamaica's African past.

Coexisting with this vibrant youth culture was a still vital older musical world, harboring "folk" forms tied to various traditional social settings that remained a part of daily life—village churches, social dances, wakes, parades, healing ceremonies, communal labor. These too were "roots" musics, although in a much less self-conscious way. And although, at the time, these so-called folk musics were spurned by many urbanizing youths, who saw them as old-fashioned, all of Jamaica's musics seemed to me to be interconnected, part of the same larger world. The rural quadrille and mento musicians I recorded in the hills of St. Ann in 1975 all knew Bob Marley personally—he had grown up in a neighboring village listening to the very music they still played virtually every weekend—and there was much excitement about the ambitious local boy, a true son of the soil just like them, who was just then starting to take the world by storm. As I continued to move between different parts of Jamaica, exploring its complex and layered social and cultural reality, I began to feel and hear more clearly how much of the old continued to live in the new.

By the time I finally felt ready to turn my focus to the sound of the city and to seek out some of its creators, more than two decades had passed. In the interim I had gained an abundance of experience in the Jamaican countryside. After spending roughly a year in a Maroon town in the mountains of the eastern part of the island, where I had shared in daily life and learned as much as I could about the unique music of that community, I had returned to Jamaica many times to explore other kinds of music, traveling widely and eventually making field recordings of traditional genres in every parish. I had learned the rudiments of Kumina drumming and had sat in on the bandu drum at ceremonies for the Kongo ancestors. I had been welcomed to Revival Zion and Poco meetings and Pentecostal services. I had learned old songs from mediums possessed by the spirits of long-departed African Bongo men. I had added my voice to the chorus at nine nights (wakes) and had joined in on guitar at quadrille dances and mento sessions. I had faced the fire at Rastafarian Nyabinghi ceremonies. I felt prepared, at last, to approach with both confidence and humility those pioneering studio musicians who years earlier had succeeded in synthesizing their varied Jamaican experiences and broader influences into a new music for their country and, as it turned out, the world.

THE WORDS AND IMAGES gathered in the following pages reflect my quest to better understand and pay respect to the flesh-and-blood musicians who, during the twentieth century in Jamaica, performed their own version of what the Haitian anthropologist Michel-Rolph Trouillot called "the miracle of creolization." Starting with what seemed to be little or nothing, they came up with more than anyone can say, literally changing the soundscape of the world. I wanted to know their own thoughts on this miracle. To my mind, the only way to approach this question was through face-to-face dialogue.

The opportunity to turn this dream into a reality came with a Guggenheim Fellowship in 2004, which provided me with the necessary support over the following year and beyond to track down a sizeable proportion of these foundational musicians in person, in the hope of engaging them in conversations of substance. In creating a list of musicians to contact, I relied on performers or other figures in the world of Jamaican music whom I had already met, the scant references to studio musicians in existing publications, and my own intuitions derived from years of listening and paying close attention to Jamaican popular music. As interviewing got under way, I also asked the interviewees to suggest other important musicians who might not yet have made it onto my list.

What constitutes a "musician" in this context is not always easily definable. I was interested first and foremost in instrumentalists who had been active in Jamaican studios during the critical years of the 1950s, 1960s, and 1970s. However, certain individuals identified primarily as singers also made significant contributions as occasional or regular instrumentalists, while some known mostly for their instrumental contributions also recorded from time to time as singers. Moreover, instrumentalists and singers also occasionally doubled as producers, and the opposite could also occur (though less often)—a person known mostly as a producer might perform in an instrumental or vocal role. In keeping with this fluidity, this book includes both instrumentalists and singers, as well as a handful of exceptional producers who are widely acknowledged for the creative ideas they brought to the studio. However, by choice, I have featured a preponderance of instrumentalists. Also appearing are a smaller but still substantial number of recording artists who worked almost entirely as singers. Among these singers are some who never played any instruments in recording sessions. The individuals in the latter category were included because they were credited by many of the musicians interviewed as important songwriters or arrangers, or because I was aware that they had played prominent roles of various other kinds in popular music and had regularly attended and observed studio sessions during critical periods in the music's development. Finally, to give a sense of the interconnectedness of Jamaican music as a whole, I have included alongside these professional musicians and singers a number of traditional musicians I have recorded and photographed over the years, whose musical and social worlds overlap to varying degrees and in numerous ways with the musical experiences and repertoires of these same session musicians.

Once I had tracked them down, I found that the studio musicians whose images appear here were more than ready to talk. Most were quick to express their frustration at the neglect from which they had suffered and eager to set the record straight by testifying to the way things had really worked in the studios in the old days. Both they and I knew that the credit they deserved was overdue. Beyond our shared wish to correct the record, I wanted to engage these artists in a serious dialogue about the meaning of the new music they had fashioned in the studios. In their view, where did it really come from? What were their earliest musical experiences, and what kinds of music were they exposed to while growing up? What were they thinking while bringing new forms of music into being in the studios? What about their music mattered most to them? In interviews that lasted between one and four hours, I tried to elicit (or simply keep pace with) their memories and thoughts on the creative "miracle" to which they had contributed, or any other aspect of their careers they deemed especially important.

MOST OF THE PHOTOGRAPHS that appear in this book were taken immediately after the interviews from which the juxtaposed texts were extracted. When I look at them, they speak to me of the palpable conviction running through these musicians' words. Most represent self-posed portraits taken on the spur of the moment—though, as I see it, these were special moments produced by the mutually satisfying exchange of thoughts that had come before.

Of course, only a tiny fraction of what these musicians discussed with me can be reproduced here. In selecting verbatim passages to go with the photographs, I aimed for what seemed to me high points—statements delivered with particular passion and personal conviction. The points made in these passages recur in many of the interviews and would seem to reflect widely held views among Jamaica's foundational studio musicians. Here I weave these brief individual statements together in a particular order calculated to create a kind of larger conversation that tacks between interconnecting points along a continuum of shared memories and understandings.

The texts accompanying the photographs in this book represent excerpts from interviews I myself conducted (or in some cases, songs I recorded in traditional contexts). All texts are verbatim (except for the bracketed passages), though they have been edited to make them more readable. The texts are in Jamaican English, but many of them also incorporate, to varying degrees, elements from Patwa (Jamaican Creole). I have borrowed a variety of nonstandard spellings commonly used by Jamaican "dialect" writers to indicate differences from "standard" (or metropolitan) English speech.

Each interview excerpt is supplemented with two additional features intended to provide the reader with a bit of background on the interviewee: 1) examples of what I call "standout tracks," and 2) a capsule summary containing very basic biographical information.

The "standout tracks" represent examples of recordings on which the interviewee played, sang, or otherwise performed, and which I see as somehow special. I limited myself to two such tracks per interviewee. ("Standout tracks" are provided for traditional musicians only in the rare instances in which they are known to have ventured into a studio and made recordings that were released at some point.) The criteria for selection varied, and sometimes were purely subjective. Some tracks were major hits. Some contain original versions of what were to become perennial "riddims" (backing tracks used for many later versions). Some exemplify innovative trends or critical stylistic shifts. Some were pointed out to me by interviewees as recordings of which they themselves were particularly proud. And some I selected simply because they appeal to me personally. In no way should any of them be taken to be the "best" tracks in the career of the individual in question.

The very idea of representing each of these amazingly prolific musicians and singers with only two examples might seem absurd. (Most of the musicians included in this book, even those who have received the least attention for their contributions, have played on hundreds or thousands of recordings; by some estimates, the team of Sly Dunbar and Robbie Shakespeare, to take two musicians who *have* achieved fame, have played on or produced over two hundred thousand records.) If you have listened to a good amount of Jamaican music, chances are that you have already heard most or all of the session musicians featured in this book. In fact, since studio sessions in the early days were so poorly documented, it is often impossible to tell with certainty who the individual musicians are on a particular recording. The "standout tracks" listed in the following pages, for which the contributing musicians have been identified with a high degree of certainty, are intended simply as pointers. Listeners already familiar with Jamaican music are likely to recognize many of these recordings from the titles; others may use them as a starting point to explore further the individual contributions of these originators of Jamaican music. Careful Internet searches by name of even the least-heralded session musicians appearing in this book will quickly reveal some additional tracks on which they are known to have played, and I encourage readers to use this method to seek out their work. (For additional listening suggestions, see the appendix titled "Recommended Listening" near the end of the book.)

Each capsule summary provides a few lines of background information. When known, the following information (except in the case of a few of the traditional musicians) is presented: instrument(s) (including voice) for which the individual is (or was) known; year of birth (and if applicable, death); period during which he or she first became active in recording or professional performing (or in the case of nonprofessional musicians, in performing in traditional musical events); recording or performing groups of which he or she was at some point a member (not an exhaustive listing); and general musical roles for which he or she was known (e.g., session musician, lead singer, harmony singer, producer). These brief capsule summaries are intended to help the reader quickly fit these important contributors, many of whom have unjustly been consigned to anonymity, into the larger picture of Jamaican music.

As we follow the flow of ideas, some of which appear and reappear in various guises throughout the book, we become privy to what these musicians see as the true sources and key properties of their music. Music, we learn, is for them an important conduit to an unwritten past, a means of communion with the ancestors. It is a carrier of spiritual power, a container of "magic" (as guitarist and singer Bobby Aitken puts it, music is *itself* a spirit). Music is something from deep within, something "inborn" and "in the blood" (as drummer Horsemouth Wallace puts it, something first experienced in the womb)—something that can suddenly and spontaneously "come out" of people when the time is right. Music is fundamentally a matter of "feel" (intuition and sensation); and because it relies so heavily on intuition, it offers a natural platform for experimental and creative impulses. Music is also fundamentally about "feeling" (emotion); and when feelings are painful, it becomes a healing balm. Music functions in the material world as a crucial means of economic survival, yet is fundamentally about love for one's fellow human beings and a sense of community rather than commerce. Music serves as a barometer of human suffering and a measure of social conscience that remains ever sensitive to the enormity of Jamaica's founding sin—the enslavement and attempted dehumanization of an entire people—and its painful echoes in the present. It is a privileged vehicle for messages of all kinds, a powerful voice of and for the people. It is a bearer of warnings and prophecy. It is a cry for freedom and social justice. And, we learn, music is much more than all of this. It is, when all is said and done, an irreducible and essential part of the flow of life in Jamaica. When we view it with a wide-angle lens that takes in the broad array of music makers and genres brought together in this volume, we see that the old and the new, the rural and the urban, the "traditional" and the "popular," are all integral to this irrepressible flow.

IF THERE IS TO BE a last word in this book, it belongs to the musicians, the original crafters and performers of sounds that, transformed but still recognizable, now circulate around the globe. But, as these musicians themselves might remind us, there is always more to a story than any single telling, or series of tellings, can capture. Some seeking to explain the "miracle" of Jamaican popular music might choose to focus not on the session musicians, but on the ingenuity of the studio engineers who interacted with and influenced the playing of these musicians; at a later point, these engineers took the raw materials created by the musicians and enhanced them with ideas of their own, eventually conjuring entirely new sonic worlds and musical aesthetics through the creation of electronically manipulated "dub" mixes, and in the digital dancehall era, radical new configurations of synthesized sounds. Others might wish to highlight the contributions of the crews who developed the complex and innovative sound system culture that has helped to spread Jamaican music around the world, or the vocalizing deejays who have added yet another tremendously influential dimension by regenerating the verbal artistry that has long been a prominent part of Jamaica's vigorous oral culture in the new context of mass-mediated performances. One could even argue for the critical importance of the creative entrepreneurship and risk taking of the "producers," without whom, after all, the enterprise could not have gotten off the ground either; some of these energetic businessmen also helped to shape their "products" in important ways, at times deciding what to record, how to record it, and what to release. All of these parties—sometimes in overlapping roles—played their parts. Creativity, after all, is not exclusive to "artists" (which, in Jamaican musical parlance, most often refers to singers) or "musicians" (players of instruments). But, in the written history of Jamaican popular music, the *musicians* remain, paradoxically and regrettably, the most unsung of all.

There are yet other portions of the proverbial half that has never been told that cannot be given equal time here, though these too are deserving of attention. Although the testimonies in this book occasionally point to sources of musical inspiration from beyond Jamaica, the primary focus stays on local roots and concerns. Once again, this is because I selected passages in which points were made emphatically; and these musicians tended to become particularly animated and to speak with special conviction when discussing ways in which they felt their music was specifically Jamaican. Yet Jamaica has never been closed to the rest of the world. If one were to draw on other interviews (or indeed, other sections of those excerpted in this book), it would be possible to construct a view rather different from what is presented here—one oriented more toward North American or other foreign influences than indigenous sources. This view has value as well. Make no mistake: Jamaica's session musicians always have been cosmopolitan in spirit, open to the wider world and ready to take from it as needed. And they have continued to look outward. Indeed, whether for artistic or economic reasons, many of them have become world travelers. To get a good sense of this, one need only consider how far I myself had to journey to find some of them. This project brought me not just to Jamaica, but also to London, Birmingham, New York, Miami, Boston, Philadelphia, Washington, D.C., Chicago, Los Angeles, San Francisco, Toronto, Montreal, and elsewhere.

But sometimes it is necessary, when searching for answers, to go back to where it all started. In this case, that is where an essential part of the half that remains to be told can still be found. And many of the thousands of non-Jamaican singers and players of instruments who have carried the flame of Jamaican music around the world, I think, would agree. For no matter how much they have done to make this music their own, lending their own words and giving their own hearts to it, something crucial remains of its original spark—something without which their own creations would be diminished. In much the same way, without the words and the meditations of the actual originators of Jamaican music, our understanding and appreciation of what has become one of the world's most influential musics would be greatly diminished. By listening to the originators, whose words and images grace these pages, and by remembering the inestimable portion they contributed, we help to keep the flame they long ago ignited burning bright.

Words and Images

Street musician who identified himself as "Haile Selassie III." Port Maria, St. Mary, Jamaica, 2005

Lammy Palmer & Emmanuel Palmer

All of us is Maroon* who scattered from [the] English. Dem deh man [the "first-time" Maroons who fought against the British in the eighteenth century] a mad Jehovah God himself!†—Jehovah God who rule those man, Jehovah God who lead those man, who teach those man. [Singing]:

Guinea bird-oh, seh you gone home-eh
Sa Leone Guinea bird-oh, poor me Guinea bird-oh
Guinea man-oh, poor me Guinea bird-oh
Woy-oh, seh me a fallaline-oh [wanderer, stranger]
Guinea bird-oh, me come from Guinea Coast-oh
Guinea bird-oh, me come from Guinea Coast-oh

- **Drums, vocals**
- **(Lammy: c. 1940–2012)**
- **(Emmanuel: c. 1938–2012)**
- **Active from the 1950s**
- **Maroon Kromanti master drummers**

*Maroons: enslaved Africans who escaped and formed their own free communities in the interior of the island. Their present-day descendants maintain four semiautonomous communities in the hills of Jamaica. *Kromanti* is the name of the African-based spiritual and musical tradition in the three eastern Maroon communities of Moore Town, Scot's Hall, and Charles Town.

†Meaning, those original Maroons were so spiritually powerful that they used to drive God himself crazy.

Moore Town, Portland, Jamaica, 2008

Alerth Bedasse

Tom the Sebastian* have one of de best sound system, like Coxsone.† Tom the Sebastian deh *far* ahead of Coxsone. All you hear dem talking about Coxsone, I can tell you dat! Because, to be frank, I used to go out and play a nighttime, Saturday nighttime, for Mr. [Ivan] Chin‡ too. I play whole night, and get pay. I was a sound operator also [for] Mr. Chin. And he would send me to handle de whole thing. [We play] anything [on the set]. We mix—just a mix of calypso, waltz, everything. We can play everything—jazz and all dat. You can play everything what's happening. You mix dem. They [the sound systems] used to play a lot of my songs. When they would go fe play all "Night Food," man—oh!—sometime you hear "Night Food" blasting down de road. Oh yeah! They had to do it [i.e., play it on the sound systems]. Because de public want it. Is what de public want, they give de public.

Standout Tracks

Alerth Bedasse and the Calypso Quintet, "Night Food" (1952); Alerth Bedasse and Chin's Calypso Sextet, "Big Boy and Teacher" (1956)

- **Vocals, guitar, banjo, percussion**
- **(1928–2007)**
- **Active from the 1940s**
- **Member of Chin's Calypso Sextet**
- **Lead singer, session musician**

*Tom the Great Sebastian: one of the most prominent of the early Jamaican sound systems, founded in Kingston by Thomas Wong c. 1950.

†Coxsone: Clement Seymour Dodd ("Sir Coxsone Downbeat"), owner of the renowned Downbeat sound system and famous record producer who launched Studio One.

‡Ivan Chin: early producer of commercial mento recordings in Kingston during the 1950s, who also owned a small sound system.

Kingston, Jamaica, 2005

Arthur Robinson (Bunny)

I tried to make as much [of] the R and B, but not *exactly* the foreign one. Not exactly. Because me and Skully did de R and B, and we kind of mek it off of our own, but a little touch of the R and B style. But not exactly like the foreign style completely. During dem time it was pure R and B we going into. And we did about three tune, four tune, like dat. I could remember, the first R and B name [singing], "Well, my baby has left me, and gone away—well, my baby has left me, and gone astray." That was the R and B style. But you can see that was ina our own styling.

Standout Tracks

Simms and Robinson, "End of Time" (1953); Mellow Cats and Count Ossie, "Another Moses" (1960)

- **Vocals**
- **(1935–)**
- **Member of Simms and Robinson; Bunny and Skully**
- **Active from the early 1950s**
- **Lead singer, session vocalist**

Kingston, Jamaica, 2005

Cecil Campbell (Prince Buster)

Oh, man—[rhythm and blues is] not de root, man. No, it cyaan be de root. We had a music before rhythm and blues. It's just that [Coxsone and Duke Reid* use] whatever tricks dem work mek de people feget dem national music and adapt to de American rhythm and blues deh. It just coat de society. Everybody waan look like Yankee. *No,* it couldn't be de root. De root a come from dung deh so [i.e., the downtown ghettos, literally, "down there"]. You see de word "national"?—[it means] dung deh so. [It was] before rhythm and blues! *Before* rhythm and blues. But they a point uptown† now, and I a seh, "dung so." I will tell you the truth. I don't waan hit rhythm and blues too hard. I tell a lot of people, I love it. [But] I just had to get rid of it. Because I couldn't go weh I waan go if it was still in power. But I love blues, I love jazz. De chief ting to realize [is that Jamaican popular music is] coming out of Poco, de mento, de Buru. *Dat* is weh de root deh. If de words deh weh me use, weh I identify wid, is Patwa, dat's weh de root deh. So I love it [rhythm and blues]. And it inspire me. I learn tings from blues. But dat's not de root dat, man.

Standout Tracks

Prince Buster, "They Got to Come" (1962); Prince Buster, "Wine and Grine" (1969)

- **Vocals, percussion, production, songwriter**
- **(1938–)**
- **Active from the late 1950s**
- **Lead singer, producer**

*Arthur "Duke" Reid: owner of an early sound system in Kingston during the 1950s called Trojan, one of the main rivals of Coxsone's Downbeat sound system; Duke Reid later became a record producer and opened the famous Treasure Isle studio.

†In Kingston's social geography, "uptown" refers to the more affluent northern section of the city, and "downtown" to the poorer southern section. The dividing line between the two is generally considered to be Cross Roads (although today some draw the line farther north at Half Way Tree).

Kingston, Jamaica, 2005

Owen Gray

We were trying various different style of sound and whatever. And ska comes around in a way that I don't think I myself really know how—just going into it, and listening to certain thing, and placing it. That's how it go. Honestly, I just sing. I just write songs and sing. And so the *musicians* them would be more knowledgeable, to bring [those] sounds in—the musicians them, I would say. *Not* the artists [i.e., the singers], [but] the *musicians* them. Because they are the most important part of the music scene. To be honest with you, it's the *musicians.* It is the musicians. We are to give them credit. Because they have talk in it too. They say, "Why don't [you] try it this way?" or "Why don't you do it this way? Listen to this and see how it sounds, and see if you can catch on [to] it." It *is* the musicians. That's what I would say. I would give them thanks and praise every time. It *is* the musicians who created the ska. We [singers] only *wrote* the songs. We only wrote the songs to fit that riddim. But the *musicians* are the ones who *created* the ska sounds. [With] rocksteady, it's the same thing—the musicians.

Standout Tracks

Owen Gray, "On the Beach" (1961); Owen Gray, "Bongo Natty" (1975)

- **Vocals**
- **(1939–)**
- **Active from the late 1950s**
- **Lead singer**

Wolverhampton, England, 2010

Jerome Haynes (Jah Jerry)

Is I carry de ska. I was de "ska man." Because no one can play like me. Coxsone used to bring dem record, because him used to do farmwork. And him bring down nice kind of music—rhythm and blues. Him used to bring it from America. Is a different beat from ska. It was not ska. In de old time, that was de old-time [rhythm-and-blues] beat. But now I carry ska. Is a different ting. I don't know [what gave me the inspiration to do that]. [Prince] Buster dem ben waan cut out de white bredda deh weh come give de problem. Dem used to call him "King of Rock"—Elvis Presley. And dem no like dat kind of ting, dem seh. Dem want dem own music, dem own beat. And dem tell me dat. So I say I going try and find a good ting fe we. So I find de ska. I find it in de guitar—just like magic. It's like magic, man. Because I never played it yet. I never used to play dat otherwise. Is [only] when him say him waan something different. And there we were.

Standout Tracks

Prince Buster, "They Got to Go" (1962); Maytals, "Sixth and Seventh Books" (1963)

- **Guitar**
- **(1921–2007)**
- **Active from the late 1940s**
- **Member of Val Bennett Band; Skatalites**
- **Session musician**

Kingston, Jamaica, 2005

Evan Lloyd Richards (Richard Ace)

N*obody* invented the Jamaican music. We just interpret what came out of the people's inspiration. Nobody never get up today and say, "We going mek this ting." No. Everything [was] cut right on the spot. You don't have time to go home and come back, and all dat stuff. You come a de session and everything spontaneous. De first ska record was "Sixth and Seventh Books of Moses." Toots and the Maytals was the first. I was the pianist. That was the first ska record ever made. It was the first one!—the first one to have the ska beat. Everything was a half blues before dat. That is what happened when [Coxsone] brought Toots with me. That just came out of us—a spirituality that you feel. That's de heart of it. When you watch a painting, is the feeling you get from it. That is called metaphysics. A person who can look at a key and know that A is red, G is purple—that's metaphysics. So dat is what happen at dat moment. Toots over dere listening to all those churches over dere in Trench Town—[loudly vocalizes, as if in the spirit]: "Eh, be be, be be!" Because he live right in de middle of it. And when him go so—"Eh, be be be be!"—I just [go] "ben, ben!" [on the piano]. And that was it. And then, the next person who reinforced that was Jah Jerry. Because Jah Jerry start draw dat now wid me now. And then everybody pitch in. "Sixth and Seventh Book"—that was the first authentic ska record.

Standout Tracks

Maytals, "Sixth and Seventh Books" (1963); Richard Ace, "Hang 'Em High" (1969)

- **Piano, organ, vocals**
- **(1940–)**
- **Active from the late 1950s**
- **Member of Rhythm Aces; Sound Dimension; Soul Defenders; Jah Ace and the Sons of Ace**
- **Session musician, lead singer**

Philadelphia, Pennsylvania, 2005

Ivanhoe Wilson

and Members of the Zion Hill Congregation (Bongo, Great House)

I think angel in heaven love to hear music. Dat's a part of invokement. Dat's de way you invoke, by singing. I am talking [about] singing *my* song—I call it God's song, de angels' song. When we sing dat, de spirit come closer to me, and uplift me. We all go by our Bible. We all go by our hymnbook. These thing come up and you will hear humming. If you do my work, you will hear humming, you will hear tune come to you. Dat's how it goes. And you sing it.

- **Vocals**
- **(1929–)**
- **Active from 1954**
- **Revival leader, singer**

Richmond, St. Mary, Jamaica, 2005

George Dudley (Bunny)

My mother was a church singer. They had some church they call Poco church—Revival. My mother was one of those type of singer. My grandmother was a Revivalist too. When they start to sing, they inspired me. So whenever time I appear, I sit there quietly and listen. The Revival church carry some Revival song that [were] heartbreaking—even in this time. You see deejay and all these thing? It's just a Revival song they are singing! And the same Revival song that people dem [sing] weh used to have wake, nine night, they woulda used to sing those song. So these song now are making number one hit. And de Revival people dem don't get no credit for that. They don't get no credit for that, you know. You see Negro spiritual? I love that so much. We just revive the Revival song. Because it was a song that I love. Most of the music in this time is coming from the Revival foundation. So this Revival thing, up to this time, you see everything revive, from the beginning time: "So shall it be in the beginning, so shall it be in the end." You will be hearing de ting in different style—Revival.

Standout Tracks

Bunny and Skitter, "Chubby" (1961); Count Ossie and the Mystic Revelation of Rastafari, "So Long" (1973)

- **Vocals, percussion**
- **(1939–2012)**
- **Active from the late 1950s**
- **Member of Bunny and Skitter; Mystic Revelation of Rastafari**
- **Lead singer**

Kingston, Jamaica, 2005

Rafael Griffiths[*]

and Members of the Congregation of the African Reform Church of God

We play our drum with meditation, and recall, with riddims, that anyhow you hear it play, if you even sit down, you have fe all rock youself. And if you stand up, you have fe a move. And if you even stop go a dance, as old as you may be, you have fe kick up and start do something. We have thousands of song that you don't hear yet. Some of them are hymns from hymnbooks. [We call our style] chanting. Dat is not singing, dat is chanting. You are looking in a divine world—not in this physical one that we're looking into. We're looking now through de spirit. And then things come to you. We was there *long* time before Bob Marley—long, long before Bob. It's a West African tradition. De Kumina is a West African tradition. And all these things are West African tradition. Because de African was a clever set a people.

- **Drums, vocals**
- **(c. 1935–)**
- **Active since 1950s**
- **Rastafarian drummer and chant leader**

*In gown.

Braes River, St. Elizabeth, Jamaica, 2000

Lloyd Clayton (Bro. Job, Baba Job)

Me see all de tune, hear dem sing it all pon record now. De Boney M.* dem did sing dat tune deh, and it go number one—"By the Rivers of Babylon." That tune, it was we [early Rastafarians] first sing dat tune. *We* sing dat tune when we was in de camp down a Salt Lane. We used to sing dat tune deh, "By the Rivers of Babylon." Me have all tune deh now weh me no hear none of dem no sing dat tune fe mek no record off of dat, for dem don't remember dat one deh, or did know dat one too tough. But we used to sing all dat one deh too. Nuff of de tune dem weh we hear dem record now, is we first used to sing those tune.

Standout Tracks

King Joe Francis and African Drums, "Bam Mo She" (1961); Bob Marley and the Wailers, "Revolution" (1974)

- **Buru drums**
- **(1933–2004)**
- **Active from the late 1930s**
- **Master drummer in the Buru tradition**
- **Teacher of Count Ossie**
- **Occasional session musician**

*Boney M.: vocal group based in Germany. Of mixed Caribbean background, the group was created by a German record producer in the 1970s. In 1978 they hit big with their disco version of "By the Rivers of Babylon," based on the earlier Jamaican reggae hit by the Melodians. Boney M.'s version reached number one on the charts in several European countries.

Kingston, Jamaica, 2002

J. McLaughlin

When drum start bite, man, is spiritual. [In] Back-o-Wall* days [they used to play Buru to celebrate someone's release from prison]. I go to Back-o-Wall and see Buru play—same ting [as here in Clarendon]. But we play more stylish ya. Our playing more stylish—[more] musical. [It was] *long* time [ago], man. [I] shake all de shaker, and play funde [there], man. Me go a Back-o-Wall and go play, man.

- **Drums, vocals**
- **(c. 1930–)**
- **Active from the 1950s**
- **Buru drummer and singer**

*Back-o-Wall: famous shantytown in West Kingston that was once considered one of the worst slums in the Caribbean. As a result of mass migration from rural areas during the 1950s, its population swelled to over five thousand. It was razed in 1966 to make way for an urban development project (now known as Tivoli Gardens), but is still remembered as an early hotbed of Rastafarian culture as well as a center of older African-Jamaican practices such as Kumina, Buru, and Poco.

Lionel Town, Clarendon, Jamaica, 2000

Donald Manning

Dem time deh when me a grow up, Back-o-Wall just get ina swing. We used to go round dere. We used to go which part dem play Buru, man. Me and Skully used to deh a Back-o-Wall together. Me play congo drum, man, and bass drum too—de big drum. Me play all of dem, man. Me used to go a Dungle,* down a Salt Lane, and we used to go all different beaches, and de Rastaman a play our beat. You have fe play Kumina too, you know. Believe wah me a tell you. These younger youth, dem no know nutten about Rastafari, dem a fashion dread. We call dem "bathroom dread." I'm not joking, man! Me play Kumina a Salt Lane, me and Harry T [Harry T. Powell], and James. We used to go down deh go play with Binghi. They a play Binghi and seh "Kumina!," and you have fe go play Kumina too!

Standout Tracks

Abyssinians, "Satta Masa Gana" (1969); Abyssinians, "Declaration of Rights" (1969)

- **Vocals**
- **(1940–)**
- **Active from the late 1960s**
- **Member of Abyssinians**
- **Lead singer, harmony singer**

*The Dungle (from "dunghill," meaning garbage heap): unofficial name of a large slum in West Kingston during the 1950s and 1960s of which Back-o-Wall was a part.

Miami Gardens, Florida, 2005

Herbert Armsby

Since me dead and gone
Sinner man
Since me dead and gone
Sinner man
Cock never crow a me yard
Sinner man
Cock never crow a me grave
Sinner man
When me was a living Bongo man*
Sinner man
Cock never crow a me yard
Sinner man
When me was a living jumbie man†
Sinner man
Jumbie never rock a me grave

- **Drums, vocals**
- **(c. 1948–)**
- **Active from the early 1970s**
- **Kumina drummer and singer**

*Bongo man: an African man. The term originally was used by practitioners of older African-Jamaican religions such as Kumina to identify with their African origins and later was adopted by Rastafarians as a term of pride.

†Jumbie man: ritual specialist who works with spirits ("jumbie" is a synonym for "duppy," meaning human spirit or ghost).

Spanish Town, St. Catherine, Jamaica, 1975

Winston Grennan

When you're a inborn musician, you have it already. You don't have to go through no long process. I was a inborn musician. Because I was in me mother belly listening to it. And then when I born, I come out, I realize, "Yo, I'm close to it." So I know then dat I could do all different things. Once you know de roots, once you have de roots, and understand what is de roots, and what de roots really mean, then certain tings no hard to play. Many things I do, I just do it. I don't really practice dem. Sometime I flash back [in memory] from Lighthouse, right back to over Dalvey, back over to Amity Hall, and dem places [in rural St. Thomas parish]—a lot of dem places where I used to walk foot late hours a night, go through bad cow pasture, and run from cow, fe reach certain Kumina places, fe play. I used to walk, and anywhere de music is, I find it, man, and just jam. Because dat's what I always like to do. From I hear a banjo or a guitar strike, and a drum, I smell it till I find it. Me and my mother used to have a lot of fight over dat, because sometime when she looking fe me, I sneak out and gone. Sometime I come back, de door lock, I have fe sleep under de cellar, wid de dog dem, and pray no centipede or no scorpion no catch you while you sleeping.

Standout Tracks

Jimmy Cliff, "The Harder They Come" (1972); Paul Simon, "Mother and Child Reunion" (1972)

- **Drum set, vocals, trombone**
- **(1944–2000)**
- **Active from the mid-1960s**
- **Member of Caribbeats; Kid Creole and the Coconuts; Ska Rocks Band**
- **Session musician, lead singer, band leader**

Kingston, New York, 1998

Linford Brown (Hux)

I play mento, and I love mento. Now [in contemporary dancehall music] they're playing what my aunt used to play in church. They're playing a little of Kumina, and a little of Poco. My aunt was a Pocomanian. And I used to go to the church. I used to play Poco drums—"pú-ku duk, pa-ká, pa tí-ki ti, tí-ki tí-ku don." [When dancehall music started to go digital], all of a sudden I hear this, "pú-kum, a pú-ku dum, pum." That is shit we doing long time ago! My grandmother used to dance dat! So all dese ting weh dem seh is "dancehall," that's what my grandmother used to do a long time ago. We [studio musicians] could have done that years ago, if we wanted. And if you listen back, a couple of records, we have it on there. When Winston Grennan used to play [drums], him used to play Poco too. I used to play Kumina [myself]. I love Kumina. I *love* Kumina. You give me a drum, and I will tear it up [i.e., play it like crazy] too.

Standout Tracks

Ken Boothe, "Freedom Street" (1970); Jimmy Cliff, "The Harder They Come" (1972)

- **Guitar**
- **(1944–)**
- **Active from the early 1960s**
- **Member of Playboys; Mighty Vikings; Boris Gardiner Happening; Soul Vendors**
- **Session musician**

Oakland, California, 2006

Edgar Reid

We [original followers of Leonard Howell] a play de [Kumina] drum [at Pinnacle] at nights.* From Pinnacle to Sligoville is five miles. De people dem, when dem passing down, they ask us what the hell we take and knock de drum. And [they say] dat it sound five miles up on de hill where they living. They sit down at night, and is just like where they are, everything is words, words. I says, "Well, that's our telephone wires." [In] de Big Yard, it's so beautiful when de moon shining—[at] de Parade [ground]. Ah, you could able to dance around [to the music of the drums]—de kibandu and de playing kyas. You see, you carry de option so as to show de people de African culture, in song and so on. When I'm in de country, and when de people catch de myal [i.e., get in the spirit], and de drum playing, dat is when de others sing and seh [sings]: "Water muddy, Lord, we a go a river go drink water." So, when de drum a lick and so on, and [they feel] de different vibration of de drum, and when de spiritual parts come in, people dem *run* along, and you have to hold dem, because—myal—they are in de spirit.

- **Vocals**
- **(1916–1997)**
- **Active from the 1930s**
- **Lead singer and lieutenant in the early Howellite church**

*Leonard Percival Howell: generally acknowledged as the first prophet to preach the divinity of Ras Tafari [Haile Selassie], beginning shortly after 1930. Along with his followers, known as Howellites, he started a large Rastafarian commune known as Pinnacle, in St. Catherine parish, which thrived during the 1940s but was broken up by colonial police in the early 1950s. Pinnacle is widely seen as one of the key sites where cultural ideas and practices that later became fundamental to the Rastafari faith first developed.

Tredegar Park, St. Catherine, Jamaica, 1995

David Powell (Lapi)

When dem ina myal [spirit possession], dem mek up a fire, and dance round it—and *dance* round it, *dance* round it. Dem mek up a big fire, like you see all dem Rasta people a go and [do nowadays at Nyabinghi ceremonies]. Dat is first-time, you know. Me go up deh when me was a little boy, go up deh, and me play drum deh. Dem have dem special song weh dem sing. Dem seh dem get ina myal. Dem seh duppy di-deh so [were right there]. Duppy di-deh, and dem seh dem waan get out de duppy now, so dem get away and mek up dem fire and start sing and play Jonkonnu and scatter rum, all dem someting deh!—scatter rum round de fire. Dem mek up dem little fire round deh, and dem jump around, jump around, jump around, and dash 'way dem rum and sing.

- **Drums, vocals**
- **(1930–)**
- **Active since 1940s**
- **Gumbe drummer, Jankunu [Jonkonnu] drummer, nine-night drummer**

Nain, St. Elizabeth, Jamaica, 2005

Neville Baker, Lucille Forbes, and Company

Oh, maam-oh, maam-oh, come ring de bell-oh
Oh, peace-oh, come in-oh
Oh, death-oh, death-oh, death a come-oh
Oh, maam-oh, come in-oh
Oh, maam-oh, maam-oh, come ring de bell-oh
Oh, peace-oh, come in-oh
Oh, death-oh, death-oh, death a come-oh
Oh, maam-oh, come in-oh

- **Drums, percussion, vocals**
- **Active since the 1950s**
- **Neville Baker: gumbe drummer, singer**
- **Lucille Forbes (facing Baker): maam (song leader in Jankunu [Jonkonnu] tradition)**

Lacovia, St. Elizabeth, Jamaica, 1991

Vira Brown

Amba* ina yard
Amba-oh, amba-oh
Roll de amba
Amba-oh, amba-oh
Amba jege
Amba-oh, amba-oh
Deat' gone a yard
Amba-oh, amba-oh
Den you roll de gumbe drum
Amba-oh, amba-oh
Oh, duppy deh a me yard
Amba-oh, amba-oh

Oh, gyal, a deat' deh a me door
Amba-oh, amba-oh
Gyal, you roll de gumbe
Amba-oh, amba-oh
Gyal, a deat' a me yard
Amba-oh, amba-oh
Gyal, a deat' deh a me door
Amba-oh, amba-oh
Gyal, you roll de amba-oh
Amba-oh, amba-oh
Gyal, you roll de amba-oh
Amba-oh, amba-oh

We have de shéke [rattle] fe shake, when we singing—something like seed in deh. We have it fe shake, and use de board fe beat, fe knock—[what we call] kwata, and de gumbe [drum]. And then you get de good sound of everything. Me go a *plenty* place, from here to Windsor, Balaclava, Maroon Town, Black River, Braes River, Santa Cruz. Only in de [home] district [do they allow spirits to take possession of dancers]. Myal lick after dem [when we perform outside], but dem no dance it. Dem no dance none. Dem control it. When you go out wid [the Jankunu],† dem cyaan dance [myal] out deh. Dem dance it ina de district ya now, but when you go out pon big way, on de parade, [and] myal tek dem, dem cyaan dance it, when we go out wid de Jankunu. We have fe just cool it off. If you have a little rum, you give dem, or one glass of cool water, and it cool dem down.

- **Vocals**
- **(c. 1930–)**
- **Active from the 1940s**
- **Maam (song leader in Jankunu [Jonkonnu] tradition)**

*Amba: translucent spherical object used for spiritual divination in Gumbe Play ceremonies in western Jamaica.

†Jankunu: here referring specifically to the spiritually charged house headdress worn during Christmas ceremonies held for the ancestors in parts of western Jamaica.

Coker, St. Elizabeth, Jamaica, 2004

Derrick Bell (Gus)

I am the master for the Buru drum. "Buru" mean de whole of de population, de whole family, tradition of de whole nation—ancestors to ancestors. I'm the leader; I get it from the old master [of the Buru drum]. Those songs, I born come see those songs. And when those start sing, those song, in de grand market night,* you feel that impression, water run off you eye, you have to cry. Every grand market night, I cry. Because is those tradition within the ancestors. De ancestors dem, is dem into me, and de more de drum plays, de more I feel de courage, de sweetness, and water just run out of my eye.

- **Buru drums**
- **(c. 1955–)**
- **Active from the 1960s**
- **Master drummer in the Buru tradition**

*Grand market night: traditional Jamaican celebration on Christmas Eve that draws large crowds. Attractions typically include large numbers of vendors, displays of toys for children, music, firecrackers, carousing, and general merriment.

Old Harbour Bay, St. Catherine, Jamaica, 2004

George Matthews (Kwabi)

Is de Buru drum me learn first [before learning Kumina]—de repeater. A me a de master fe dat. Me sat down and hear how de older head one dem play, and me adopt de principle. And me have nuff understanding, and have nuff culture, to understand how to play dem. I up and down with the older head dem. August time, Christmas time, and Easter time, I play with dem.

- **Buru drums, Kumina drums**
- **(1936–)**
- **Active from the 1950s**
- **Master drummer in the Buru tradition**

Lionel Town, Clarendon, Jamaica, 2000

Estavan Callaghan

Hear how de songs goes: if we see a man doing something, we just look pon him and build a song. It come like de reggae, how those boy have deejay, dey woulda see a ting going on, and dem just use it as a deejay. Well, a same way. The spirit of the Buru is just dancing—playing and dancing. That's the spirit of the Buru. Is something keep de place lively.

- **Buru drums**
- **(1929–)**
- **Active from the 1930s**
- **Master drummer in the Buru tradition**

Hayes, Clarendon, Jamaica, 2000

Derrick Morgan

We used to dance off mento music, like [sings]: "What is catty?—Big Boy ask." Those type of songs we grow up on—"tún-dup, tun-yún dop, tun-yún-dop, tun-yún-dop, n-yéng-e." That is what *we* grow up on—banjo playing wid a pick bass [i.e., a plucked bass—a bass lamellophone, or "finger piano"]. They call it the rumba box. That's what *we* grow up on, from my age down—people in my age. At every bar, every pub you went, man would sit dere [and listen], in Kingston. All de bars have mento. You used to have people sit at dem rum bar [playing mento]. Because when dem play de song, you give dem drink. You know, they don't work for money, they just work for drink. It's sweet! It's sweet, man! Mento music was nice. Very nice. [I] listen to dem, and playing, and de *banjo,* and dem have dat fife to tek de solos and ting—something like what de Jonkonnu dem going around wid now, and blowing de same ting.

Standout Tracks

Derrick Morgan, "Forward March" (1962); Derrick Morgan, "Tougher Than Tough" (1967)

- **Vocals, production, songwriter**
- **(1940–)**
- **Active from the late 1950s**
- **Lead singer, producer**

Freetown, Clarendon, Jamaica, 2008

Headley Bennett (Deadly Headley)

Dat is our music—Jamaican. Mento is Jamaican music—original, you know. Trinidadian is calypso. Mento is Jamaican. Don't care what we do, as Bob Marley say, "Feel it in de one drop"—we have to go back to mento. Even de youth dem today, wid dis present dancehall music—is mento! Everything coming from mento, man. De ska is not really our music. De only difference is dat we change de beat—we add to de American march time.

Standout Tracks

Bob Marley and the Wailers, "Nice Time" (1967); Bob Marley and the Wailers, "Ride Natty Ride" (1978)

- **Saxophone**
- **(1931–)**
- **Active from the 1950s**
- **Member of Sound Dimension**
- **Session musician**

Kingston, Jamaica, 2005

Freedom Mento Band

Freedom
Freedom
Freedom ina Africa
Freedom
Freedom
Freedom all over the world
Freedom
Freedom
Freedom ina Jamaica
This is what we hoping for
To let you know we are free

- **Vocals, banjo, fife, rumba box, drums, percussion**
- **Active since 1990**

Glengoffe, St. Catherine, Jamaica, 2002

Radcliffe Bryan (Dougie)

Reggae] is indigenous. It's indigenous. It was created in Jamaica by Jamaicans. It came out of nowhere except Jamaica. It came out of brilliant minds from Jamaica. Reggae—the rhythmic pattern of reggae—has a lot to do with mento. Because, you see, for a mento rhythm, you would have the banjo or the guitar people playing. We grow up with these music forms. So it was not a difficult transformation. If that rhythm came up [while playing in the studio], the tempo got there, then something would *click* in your head. And then you would play this thing. And then, after you played it, you would say, "Damn, where did I hear this from?" And then you'd go pon it and say, "Oh, I must have heard it [before]—yeah, is a mento rhythm." You'd play it, because you hear it. You'd hear it in your head, you'd feel it, and then you'd play it. That kind of rhythm was always there, because you been hearing it all over.

Standout Tracks

Dave Barker and Ansel Collins, "Double Barrel" (1970); Bob Marley and the Wailers, "Cheer Up" (1970)

- **Guitar, vocals**
- **(1947–)**
- **Active from the mid-1960s**
- **Member of Immortals; Sensations; Revolutionaries**
- **Session musician, lead singer, session vocalist**

Portmore, St. Catherine, Jamaica, 2005

Kew Park Mento Band

Me seh cut munu,* cut munu, cut de munu
Wai-oh, cut you munu
Cut munu, cut munu, cut munu
Wai-oh, cut you munu
Me seh little munu, big munu, same munu
Wai-oh, cut you munu
Ten pound ten fe cut de munu
Wai-oh, cut you munu
You wheel and you wind and you dub de munu
Wai-oh, cut you munu
Three pon top, two underneath
Wai-oh, cut you munu
Cut, me little gyal, mek I cut you munu
Wai-oh, cut you munu
Cut, cut, cut you munu
Wai-oh, cut you munu
Little munu, big munu, same munu
Wai-oh, cut you munu

Standout Tracks

Kew Park Mento Band, "Mussu" (2000); Kew Park Mento Band, "Peanut Vendor" (2000)

- **Vocals, banjo, fife, guitar, rumba box, percussion**
- **Active from 1990**

*Munu: old term for female genitals, "cut munu" referring to sexual penetration.

Rat Trap, Westmoreland, Jamaica, 2002

Jackie Robinson

You must remember dat mento is a Jamaican art form. Calypso [is] Trinidadian, but mento is Jamaican. So it kind of makes sense that, when you listen to reggae, you hear some little influences of mento in some of de songs them—or most of de song—riddim-wise. Most mento songs tell a story about somebody, or some incident that happened. And then we had another ting that we call quadrille. So all those influence is in our reggae music. You can't get away from it. How somebody could talk about reggae and don't realize that there is a connection? Reggae music don't have anything to do with R and B, except if we cover R and B songs and we use the reggae rhythm—meaning that we sing the tune, and we sing the R and B words and the melody. But when it come to de music side of that, de riddim is strictly Jamaican. This is my personal opinion. Our reggae music is strictly Jamaican. De riddim don't have nutten to do wid anything from outside. Reggae [is] just a progression from wah we did a do wid de mento, and ska. And then, wid de rocksteady, we just put de organ—de organ shuffle—in, and the guitar playing this rhythm. And then it name "reggae." I was dere. Nobody can't tell you definitely seh it was *this* person who [first] say, "Yeah man, we have fe call dis ting 'reggae.'" Nothing like that. It's just *totally* making music, and it just totally happen by accident. Nobody coulda never plan something like reggae music. How could anybody plan it? I mean, God [could plan it]—yeah. But not human beings.

Standout Tracks

Pioneers, "Long Shot Kick de Bucket" (1969); Pioneers, "Time Hard" (1972)

- **Vocals**
- **(1951–)**
- **Active from the late 1960s**
- **Member of Pioneers**
- **Lead singer, harmony singer**

Pembroke Pines, Florida, 2005

Owen Emmanuel (Count Owen)

Every time I hear some of these so-called modern riddims, I say to myself, "That is mento!" I hear mento in it. I hear Kumina in it. I hear the old riddims in it. But they come back as new. Trust me. The music goes round and round. It comes right back again. It "revolutes." Not everything is totally original. There are aspects of it that is quite old. But you touch on it in the modern technology, and it's new to a new phase of people—all over—*brand-new*. But frankly speaking, it was here. I hear mento every day in some of these modern dancehall music. I hear mento in it. I hear Kumina in it. Yeah man.

Standout Tracks

Count Owen and His Calypsonians, "Lawd Some Man Could a Smart" (1959); Count Owen, "Rookumbine" (1964)

- **Vocals, guitar**
- **(1934–)**
- **Active from the mid-1950s**
- **Lead singer**

Kingston, Jamaica, 1999

Stanley Hunter (McBeth)

I do some quadrille record for Joe Gibbs.* But I can't remember de year. [That was my] first experience [recording]. Somebody tell him about me, seh McBeth dem can play quadrille. So him come from Town and seh him would like some quadrille music. So, me and six musician go to Kingston and play it for him, at his studio. Him come for me wid his car. And we went there and play for him. [The session lasted] not fully [a] day—[just a] few hours. We as the musician decided what to play. Quadrille we did play for him. I [sometimes] play at club place in Kingston. I play at Club Havana already. Banjo me play all de while, right *straight* through, till now. But I guess I am not so brilliant on de banjo now as first-time. Because I don't do much of de leading part now. I used to do dat, man—melody. But after I start to play wid a certain set of saxophonist, they were so good that I don't have to do no picking ting. Just strum me strum de banjo with dem.

Standout Tracks

McBeth Orchestra, "Eighteenth Century Rhumba" (c. 1973); "Twentieth Century Mento" (c. 1973)

- **Banjo**
- **(1922–)**
- **Active from the 1930s**
- **Member of McBeth and His Orchestra; Happy Six**

*Joe Gibbs: Joel Gibson, record producer active between the 1960s and his death in 2008.

Highgate, St. Mary, Jamaica, 2005

Kenneth Lara (Lord Laro)

When I came to Jamaica [from Trinidad], the mento was the music of Jamaica. And to me, mento was dying. Nobody was talking about mento again. And I say, I have to bring back the mento. And I took me guitar and start practicing home. And there the words came—how I went to a dance last night, and I was feeling tight, and the dance start to play, and the whole dance floor break away, and how was a sweet disco mento rockers—bringing the mento to the reggae now, to the calypso, and bringing this new form. The song really start off with the real mento—just mento guitar—and then just fall right into the hardcore reggae. At that time it was. Today it's considered soft reggae. But in them days it was the hardcore reggae—the bass and drums, and the skanking. And that took the dancehall right so.

Standout Tracks

Lord Laro, "Foreign Press" (1976); Lord Laro, "Reggae Mento Rockers" (1977)

- **Vocals, guitar**
- **(1940–)**
- **Active from the 1950s**
- **Lead singer**

Rose Hall, St. James, Jamaica, 2002

Stanley Beckford (Stanley Turbyne)

I were choir leader in my church. I were choir leader. That time we used to sing quartets, trio, duets, and all those type of song. That nice, you know!—when the whole group and you a sing it. Sweet! Yeah man! So I go to church because I can't tek a dead church. Fe go ina church fe just sit down so—no, man. The Bible said you must mek a joyful noise unto the Lord. Sing unto Him, pray, with a new song. And it is so nice to Him—so presentable to Him. You have some church weh you go, you cyaan seh, "Praise the Lord!"—dem run you out, seh you a fanatic spirit. But I love to go to church when me know seh church hot. That's my lover.

Standout Tracks

Starlites, "Soldering" (1975); Stanley and the Turbines, "Leave My Kisi-Loo" (1977)

- **Vocals, guitar**
- **(1942–2007)**
- **Active from the late 1960s**
- **Member of Turbines; Starlites**
- **Lead singer**

Riverdale, St. Catherine, Jamaica, 2002

Mount Peace Mento Band

John was in the spirit
On the Lord's day
He heard a voice from heaven
And this is what it said:
"I am Alpha and Omega
The beginning and the end
Behold, I live forevermore"

Behold, I live
Behold, I live
Behold, I live forevermore
Behold, I live
Behold, I live
Behold, I live forevermore

Standout Tracks

Mount Peace Mento Band, "Iron Bar" (2000); Mount Peace Mento Band, "Come Back Liza" (2000)

- **Vocals, banjo, guitar, rumba box, percussion**
- **Active from the 1970s**

Mount Peace, Hanover, Jamaica, 2005

Claudelle Clarke

People will say, "Oh, this one invented reggae, that one invented reggae." No. *No*body, none of these artists, invented reggae. You have to realize that the Revival church, the rhythm in the Revival church, it's the same as the reggae. This is how the Revival people play their music. [The studio musicians who came up with the reggae beat] would just put a heavy bass and a heavy drum set. But if you listen to the Revival people—ain't no difference with that and the reggae music. They just didn't get the credit. I listened to everybody who created reggae music. [It was] we, the church people. Reggae music come out of the church. I can tell *anybody* that, without any doubt. It came out of the church. Especially the Revival people, that's the rhythm they played in their church—the guitar, the drum. I mean, on Saturday, you'd go into Spanish Town. You'd go down in the market area. I wish somebody had recorded those people in those days. Then [people today] would compare it to the music that they're playing as reggae. And it's the same thing. Nobody should take credit for reggae music. No! Reggae music—the *rhythm*—came from out of the church. And I will tell them without any doubt that before reggae became famous, that's the way how the Revival people played their music.

Standout Tracks

Prince Buster, "Shaking Up Orange Street" (1968); Claudelle Clarke, "Closer than a Brother" (1970)

- **Vocals**
- **(c. 1950–)**
- **Active from the early 1960s**
- **Lead singer, harmony singer, session vocalist**

Chicago, Illinois, 2007

Lloyd Robinson (Sarge)

Sometimes the history doesn't seems as dramatic [as it should]. Because you lived it, you figure it's just another day in your life. I think poverty is a very dangerous thing. Because you don't even get to appreciate yourself sometimes. You're so consumed with the business of making a dollar, you don't get a chance to recall the things that happened to you as you go along. Having played in the Pocomania church before, and rolled the drum and stuff like that, I guess maybe [it did affect my later playing]. Because it's a performance. You're in the church, but you're really performing. People would come up to me [in the Poco church, when I was a boy] and seh, "You sound good!" The rhythm was really *good!* And it was locking in. Because all the things I was hearing on the radio, I was doing [them on the Revival drum too]. We didn't have no [electric] bass and [trap] drum and all, but we have tambourine, and maracas, and all that kind of stuff. So, it was a rhythm section by itself anyway. So you really had a performance.

Standout Tracks

Bob Marley and the Wailers, "I'm Gonna Put It On" (1965); Sharks, "How Could I Live" (1968)

- **Drum set, vocals**
- **(1944–2015)**
- **Active from the mid-1960s**
- **Member of Sharks**
- **Session musician, harmony singer**

Queens, New York, 2010

Rev. Otis Wright

Reggae incorporate that feeling [of the gospel rhythm guitar] into that genre. So musician help each other. You listen to what the next person is playing, and for some reason, you just try to copy their style. It was one group of people closely knitted together [in Trench Town during the 1960s]. So the one common factor is music. So you find that the interest of the music, whether it was church or secular, after a while they intertwine together. Since the music was new, you could not really differentiate between who's singing gospel or reggae. If you go in the church, if you get saved now, you stay in the church and you sing gospel. And people would look to you for singing gospel music. So your interest would be really in gospel. So it was new then. A lot of stuff is trial and error.

Standout Tracks

Otis Wright, "It Will Soon Be Done" (1967); Otis Wright, "Man from Galilee" (1969)

- **Vocals, guitar**
- **(1941–2014)**
- **Active from the early 1960s**
- **Lead singer, church musician, session musician, gospel arranger**

Elmont, New York, 2010

Derrick Harriott

These guys, when they come to the studio, it's like a Revival thing, you know—Lee Scratch Perry and Clancy Eccles, and the rest of them. It's like a ritual, when you are in the studio. So they get the musicians in the spirit, right? So, I think that's where the reggae came from. I'm telling you. You'd be surprised. They just get everybody to play. They had that little thing in them that they create. They would go all about the place and create excitement with the sound system. They would bring influence, and they start playing it. People say, "Bwai [boy], dis is a new thing." But I think [it happened] that way deh actually in the studio. Not only going to do a song. They went into the studio with [a vibe] like a meeting being held on a corner, a Revival. When they went into studio, they started just that Revival thing. They got everybody in spirit. So you'd find that, as I said, the musicians start to create things according to how they acted in the studio—the jumping up, and the *stamping,* and the works!—whether they hitting some tambourine or something. And the whole vibe of the session would just turn ina nice real reggae thing going. I think that could have started reggae.

Standout Tracks

Jiving Juniors, "Over the River" (1961); Derrick Harriott, "Solomon" (1967)

- **Production, vocals**
- **(1939–)**
- **Active from the late 1950s**
- **Member of Jiving Juniors**
- **Lead singer, producer**

Kingston, Jamaica, 2004

George Fulwood (Fully)

My mother was involved in all these churches a lot, because she's from the country. She's from St. Mary [parish]. She's from the country part there, so she was involved in these churches. When you young, you don't wanna go church. But when you go to these churches, you don't really feel that way. Because there is always that music, and there is always that electrifying thing happening within the church. You see people jumping up and down, and you're looking at people, and you see dem sweating and having all these fits and dropping on the ground and people shaking. It was a big influence in my life, growing up, as a young boy—of course. Most of de young friends them that I have growing up too used to be involved with something like that. It have a big influence on us—the church. That's why we have that kind of thing within us as a player now—more of a spiritual way. Some of us still have that in us. Because it's a spiritual experience. And we were taught dat this is a gift—[to be] able to sing and able to play an instrument. You have to realize that in Jamaica, even in de school, we never have any kind of lesson that teach you about playing music. So if you want to play a music, you have to learn by yourself, where you're self-taught, or just play by ear. So it was a blessing. That's what we were told. To be able to just sing and have music come out of your mouth—of course that's a gift! So most of the players, and most singer, we consider it as a gift. And a lot of us are more spiritual.

Standout Tracks

Bob Marley and the Wailers, "Sun Is Shining" (1970); Ansel Collins, "Stalag 17" (1974)

- **Bass guitar, vocals**
- **(1950–)**
- **Active from the late 1960s**
- **Member of Rhythm Raiders; Soul Syndicate; Word, Sound and Power**
- **Session musician, lead singer**

San Clemente, California, 2006

Vincent Morgan

When you are from the country] you have a different sound. You have a different sound. I don't know [where it comes from], I really can't tell you. [But] de [Poco] drums down a gully deh so *is* a part of me. Music is my life, you know. I wasn't taught theory. So I listen. I am self-taught, and I try to hold tings. Anytime that come inside, a so me try fe hold it, try fe remember. Retention is one of de key, you know. Ear, [and] retention—two of de key ina music. If you no have good ears, and you cyaan retain what you're hearing, you don't become a good musician. If you have fe depend on de paper and all of dat—no.

Standout Tracks

Burning Spear, "Zion Higher" (1971); Wailing Souls, "Run My People" (1974)

- **Drum set, piano, organ**
- **(1950–)**
- **Active from the late 1960s**
- **Member of Soul Defenders**
- **Session musician**

Linstead, St. Catherine, Jamaica, 2005

Winston Francis (Mr. Fix It)

When you go to a nine night [death ceremony], there were professional nine-night singers, and professional moaners. I didn't know this as a kid. But when you hear these guys singing at a nine night, it's fascinating. And it's beautiful. And these guys would come and sing for the dead. And their payment would be having a good night. And for me, it's just listening to these guys. And believe it or not, years later, when I started getting into groups and all this, and singing harmony, and there was a guy called Richard Ace who actually taught me harmonies—along with Boris Gardiner and Dennis Moss [and] Tony Gregory and a few other guys—it wasn't hard. Because you learned from standing on the corner, or going to nine nights and listening to these guys singing these harmonies. And when you hear these guys, it makes you wonder, where the hell did they learn these things? Because there were no schools to teach them these things. But these guys had it down to a tee. And it was just beautiful and fascinating to listen to these singers. So without even knowing that you're learning something, you were taking in these things, which became a part of *your* thing later on.

Standout Tracks

Winston Francis, "Mr. Fix It" (1969); Winston Francis, "Let's Go to Zion" (1980)

- **Vocals**
- **(1943–)**
- **Active from the mid-1960s**
- **Member of Sheredons**
- **Lead singer**

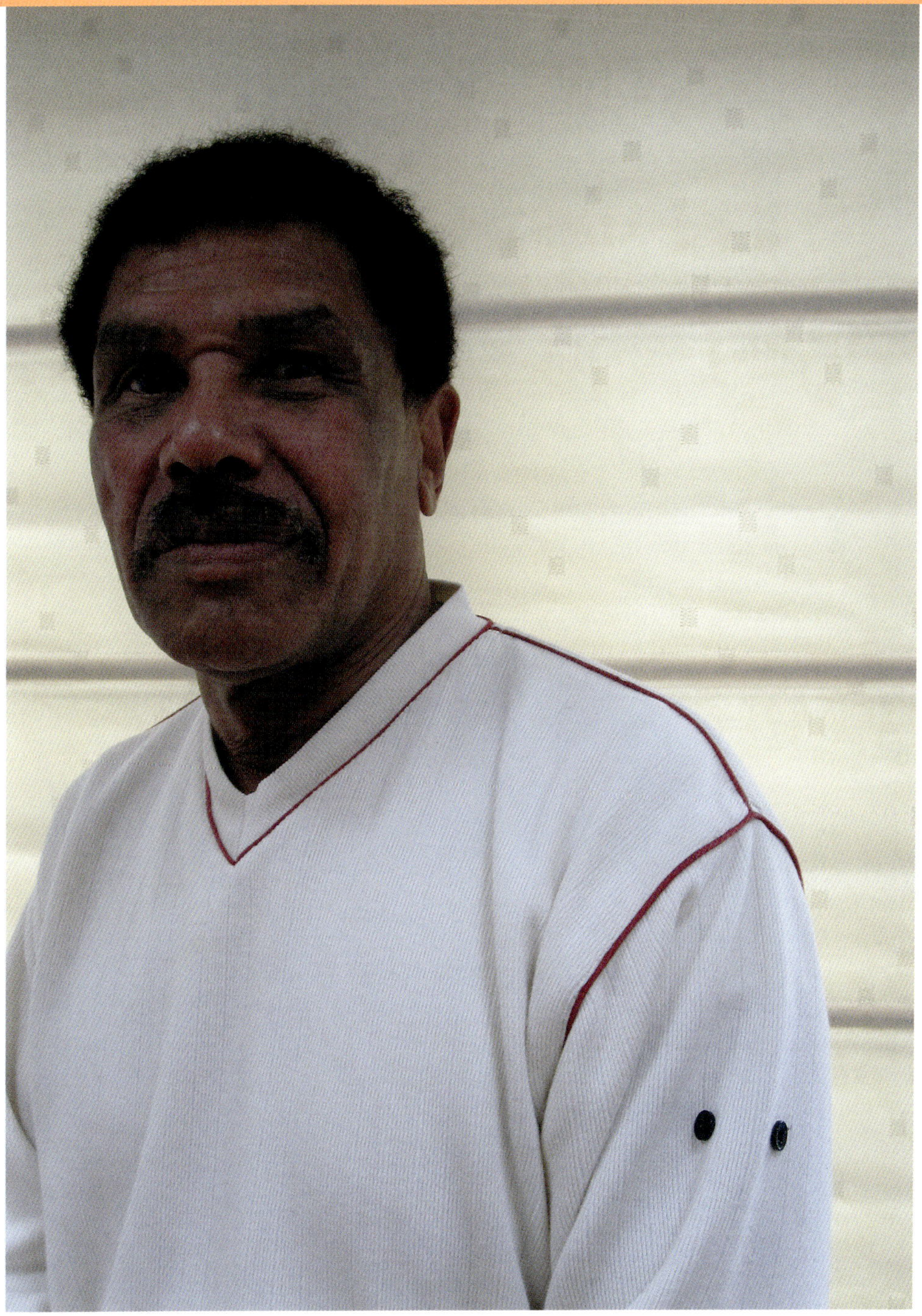

Watford, England, 2010

Bertram McLean (Ranchie)

You born ina someting, you know. Is like it be a part of you. Is what *you* want fe do wid it. If you born ina a swamp, you supposed to can swim. If you born ina de water, and you live ina de water, you supposed to can swim. So you come and you born ina dis ting weh deh-deh already, this music. You born ina dis music. You hear other music, but *born* ina dis ting. It's a part of you, in your blood. And it's just you, so it just fe come out of you. Because from you born, you been hearing it. Foreign music—we play dem. Because we have fe play dem as a part of de work. But de one weh you born and grow up ina, you going want fe do dat more. I hear all of dem—all of de music dem—nine night, and all of dem stuff deh. Because we go to set up [wakes], and we sing. It's a part of it—the whole ting. Because nine-night band play [even] now, you know. We have some now we call de "duppy band," that play at nine nights. When you hear, you don't waan leave.

Standout Tracks

On guitar: Al Brown, "Here I Am Baby" (1974); on bass guitar: Meditations, "Woman Is Like a Shadow" (1976)

- **Bass guitar, guitar, vocals**
- **(1948–2012)**
- **Active from the late 1960s**
- **Member of Skin, Flesh and Bones; Revolutionaries; Oneness Band**
- **Session musician, lead singer**

Kingston, Jamaica, 2008

Alvin Patterson (Seeco)

That's why [reggae] hit so much—it was so new and strange. And the sound was good. The sound just come up, you know. It just come up out of us. That sound just come up. I don't know, really, the direction of it. But I think it come from the drum. The drum express it. The whole thing come from the funde—the drum. The drum is the whole buildup of the reggae. I know long time it is coming from the drum. The whole music come from the drum. Drum come like the first music. A drum is the first music. Everybody have a drum, in Africa. Drum! Drum is the first music, man. So I think drum produced the reggae. It's a drum sound.

Standout Tracks

Bob Marley and the Wailers, "Time Will Tell" (1978); Bob Marley and the Wailers, "Babylon System" (1979)

- **Drums, percussion**
- **(1934–)**
- **Active from the 1950s**
- **Member of Bob Marley and the Wailers**

Kingston, Jamaica, 2005

Michael Henry (Ras Michael)

In de history of de African slaves that were brought here, we had all type of different style of drummers, and drumming style. All of dem is from Africa. So we cannot leave out one or the other. Me see [Kumina drummers] too [as a youth]. Me see dem all down a Matthews Lane. Me see dem down pon West Street, weh you used to have some people, dem call dem Pocomania—weh dem tie dem head wid a whole heap of tings, and sing, and play dem [drums], and jump up and roll and speak in tongues too, according to how their spirit is feeling within themselves. It is a African tradition. When you hear it start, as a little boy, it arouse you interest—specially me, when I did little, dem time deh. And me mother would seh she a go a meeting. And she would go, and carry me too. And then me see de people dem jump round, and then dem start dem Kumina service. Dem people deh, they have some great voices—the Africans. De Africans ina dem time deh, they had a great voice of singing. When dem start sing, dem can call *you* too. And you would hear dat call. Dem may cut some languages, and you a seh, "Hey! Weh dat?" And you see dem jump up and talk. And dem read dem Bible too, wid dem tinnen lamp. She [my mother] carry me a Revival meeting too. It's a old tradition. De whole of it is Jamaica.

Standout Tracks

Ras Michael and the Sons of Negus, "None a Jah Jah Children" (1975); Ras Michael and the Sons of Negus, "A New Name Jah Got" (1976)

- **Drums, vocals**
- **(1943–)**
- **Active from the mid-1960s**
- **Member of Sons of Negus**
- **Lead singer, master drummer in Nyabinghi tradition**

Los Angeles, California, 2006

Noel Simms (Skully, Zoot Simms, Mr. Foundation)

We playing drum a night time, and we have fe run—grab up de drum and run. Dem come, waan beat we up fe nutten at all. Dem seh both—[that we're smoking] de ganja [marijuana], and dem don't like de drum. Because dem seh de drum now draw de youth, and de youth dem come and they woulda dance off of de kete [Rastafarian repeater drum], and dem will smoke a spliff [large, cone-shaped cannabis cigarette]. So dem seh de youth dem a smoke ganja, and [there was also] de sound weh we a lick out again. Because we a sing songs fe burn down Babylon and all dem ting deh. So dem no like all dat—because we are singing [that] we want equal rights and justice. Man must have free speech. [But in the] colonial [days]—weh you think? You coulda go chat-chat up you mouth? Dem will just *box* you down and a lock you up. And you gone a prison.

Standout Tracks

Mr. Foundation, "See Dem a Come" (1966); Zoot Simms, "Small Garden" (1972)

- **Vocals, drums, percussion**
- **(1935–)**
- **Active from the early 1950s**
- **Member of Simms and Robinson; Bunny and Skully; Revolutionaries**
- **Session musician, lead singer, session vocalist**

Kingston, Jamaica, 2005

Allena Robertson (Polly)

From I was a child growing up, when they usually play de Buru, they did have a bamboo lawn, right underneath de tambrin [tamarind] tree. They usually have two type of playing dere. You had de Buru, and you had de ting dat you call de Jonkonnu. Inside de Christmas season, you have de old ancestors who die dere, what you see we march around de grave, and come around. From thence Buru been playing dere until now. Buru is real, a spirituality coming from de ancestors. Dis is a trend set from more longer time. Whether we want to, or we do not want to, we just had to let Buru prolong. It is a must. Buru cannot deteriorate. Because it is from tradition. We are *inside deep down* wid Buru. Because we *are Buru founder,* and Buru contender. So dere is no apologetic feelings from no one.

- **Vocals, percussion**
- **(c. 1945–)**
- **Active from the early 1970s**
- **Lead Buru singer**

Old Harbour Bay, St. Catherine, Jamaica, 2004

Eric MacDonald (Brother Joe)

Those days me start music. We start wid a little pan, for we don't have any drums—[me and] Ras Michael, and some more bredren. [And] Jack [Albert Hewitt] too! And after dat now, de faith start de drumming. De people dem round dem man, all de people dem dat live around de man dem, bwai, dem just accept. When we keep any time, de yard *full* of people! I build it! I see how it build. I know man weh used to build de drum. But he get old now. I saw dem, how dem build it. And we used to go down at Barry Street and go buy some peanut, and we see dem have a keg down deh, weh dem bring down de tings dem into. And I beg one. We beg de Chiney man dem two of de keg. And me seh, "Ras Michael, I going build one fe you, and one fe meself." And I just build it.

Standout Tracks

Soul Vendors, "Drum Song" (1968); Brother Joe and the Rightful Brothers, "Freedom of Life" (1978)

- **Drums**
- **(1934–)**
- **Active from the mid-1960s**
- **Member of Rightful Brothers**
- **Session musician**

Red Hills, St. Andrew, Jamaica, 2005

Albert Hewitt (Brother Jack, Pa Jack)

Most of dem drums music you hear out of Coxsone studio, is me and [Brother] Joe. The first music is "Darker Shade of Black" and "Soul Drum." Those sessions happen because we did have a demands towards the program. We did have a program going on in Jamaica name "The Lion of Judah Time." They bring over the service, wid chanting and Bible lesson. So, we did play that music fe Coxsone, fe really get a money fe fulfill the program. It was a radio program—JBC. What we bring into de people on those days, it is livity [the proper way of living], truth and right, and love—stop tief, stop murder, and stop evil. That's all that de Rastaman a deal wid, and him little herb. We no interfere wid people business otherwise. The real music in Jamaica those time is Rasta, you know. For the drums was the tool of the message. For drum and bass, it was the major thing in music. So we always tool the drums, and the drums carry nice message. And whether they want it or not, we used to chant about Rastafari and mek music. So both Peter [Tosh] and we, and Bunny [Livingston] and Bob [Marley], just chant music.

Standout Tracks

Heptones, "Equal Rights" (1968); Ras Michael and the Sons of Negus, "A New Name Jah Got" (1976)

- **Drums, percussion**
- **(c. 1940–2015)**
- **Active from the mid-1960s**
- **Member of Sons of Negus**
- **Session musician**

Temple Hills, Maryland, 2005

Cedric Myton (Cedric Congos)

My music come really out of the Nyabinghi. It's a churchical ting. When we really get deep within the music, it's all [about] the freedom for the people. It's all a spiritual atmosphere, or a spiritual awakening, or a spiritual dream. And on a whole, what we thinking about is really for the redemption of the people—even the slaves that were here from that time. For a de same one people, although a hundred year might pass, two hundred year might pass, three, four, five hundred year. Is the same one people. Is the same one generation. Is just like you and me and many more. Is just de same one generation, from dat time—our foreparents, or grandparents. So it's all a spiritual thing, it's all a churchical thing, it's all a physical thing. And it's all a musical thing.

Standout Tracks

Tartans, "Rolling Down the Street" (1966); Congos, "Row Fisherman" (1977)

- **Vocals, percussion**
- **(1947–)**
- **Active from the mid-1960s**
- **Member of Tartans; Congos**
- **Lead singer, session vocalist**

Old Harbour Bay, St. Catherine, Jamaica, 2005

Glen Adams (Capo)

Just pure experiment—that's where it lies. Reggae was just a experiment. It was just a thing, and it happening. And the people were thirsty, and wanted something different. It just came out. [The people] loved it. And they pick it up. And we become dominant in the city, recording for everybody. We have the hits all over the city. Music is very spiritual, because it's spiritual movements. You vibes is spiritual. It's a spiritual ting. If you notice, a white man, Chiney man, a Indian, all play music. And we have such a wonderful time. It's a *spiritual* ting, music. When you a musician, all tings [are] away from the world, locked out. You don't have fe even say, "I'm spiritual." You just hear it ina de music. You understand and feel it. Reggae is a forceful music. It's a spiritual music. Is like a volcano. Something ina it a bubble up, bubble up, and want to come out, and want to get the freedom, and the freedom to do it.

Standout Tracks

Glen Adams, "Hold Down Miss Winey" (1968); Bob Marley and the Wailers, "Mr. Brown" (1970)

- **Organ, piano, vocals**
- **(1945–2010)**
- **Active from the early 1960s**
- **Member of Hippy Boys; Upsetters**
- **Session musician, lead singer**

Brooklyn, New York, 2006

Bobby Aitken

Music is a heartbeat, is a spirit. If you don't have much experience of certain tings, your music limited. A man who suffers a lot always will be a great musician. He have more to offer in music. A man who suffer a lot, literally—he has more to offer in music. Because it is coming from what he *been* through—the hurts. And sometime him take it out on de music too. Sometime he takes it out on de music, and you will hear more. I'm still hurting. Because *all* these promoters that I work for, *all* of [the] music [that I did for them, I never got properly compensated or credited for].

Standout Tracks

Bobby Aitken, "Pidi Boy" (1967); Bobby Aitken (as Barry Atkins), "Jesus Name So Sweet" (1981)

- **Guitar, vocals**
- **(1933–)**
- **Active from the early 1960s**
- **Member of Caribbeats**
- **Session musician, lead singer, band leader**

Fort Lauderdale, Florida, 2005

Carlton Davis (Santa)

What people have to understand—reggae is purely a Jamaican product. No matter what people try to come and say, this type of rhythm that we're playing, if you search the history of music as far back as you can go, you cannot link [it with] anything and say, "Reggae used to be played a hundred years ago [by] these people from some mountains somewhere." Reggae music was created in Jamaica. And *I* was there. I *know*. People love to talk. So when they don't understand things, they try to put their own little fit to it. But reggae music is a Jamaican pattern that was created *there* [in Jamaica]. It just came about by musician just experimenting until, "boom," it just came—[as] Bob Marley say, "natural mystic." And people have fe understand that. The whole root—the root of the thing—is coming from *all* those general music that we've been through—the Revival ting, the Pocomania, the calypso, the mento vibe, and then Nyabinghi, the Nyabinghi Rastaman music, that drum ting. That is really where the power [is]. That is where most of de rhythm is. If you listen to reggae music, you can hear it. But it's so powerful, that motor, [that] people would start get scared. Because is a spiritual thing. Is a Jamaica ting.

Standout Tracks

Bob Marley and the Wailers, "Duppy Conqueror" (1970); Johnny Clarke, "None Shall Escape the Judgment" (1974)

- **Drum set, percussion**
- **(1953–)**
- **Active from the mid-1960s**
- **Member of Soul Syndicate; Aggrovators; Word, Sound and Power**
- **Session musician**

Washington, DC, 2006

Roy Smith (Spar)

Most of the dancehall rhythms now carry dat [gere (rural wake music) and Poco] vibe. *We* [older musicians from country areas] know dat. Dem [people in Kingston] don't know. But *we* know it all. Because we [are] from dat time, coming up. And we see the fusion, where the contrast become. And most of the dancehall vibes now [are] coming from the Kumina and the gere. Because it's a very dancey sound. It carry a mood. And it's a vibes. And if you are a true musician who creative, *all* of it is part of de culture. So we just combine it together, and see wherein it could make an effect. And it work. A so it go, man. Straight up. And if you is a person who key link with de sound, coming up from dem time deh, you can see de changes, and know de associations. It's all based from dere. This ain't no one-man thing, really. Everybody contribute. *All* the fraternity—musical fraternity—contribute to it. It's different ideas, and you get it together, and create a sound. Everybody contribute to it. It's not a one-man thing. I can step up wid this tempo, and get a groove from it. And it depends on de mood at de time. And then now, you recognize certain ting. When you recognize it now, then you just say, "yeah," and put it to the test. So, to say any one person responsible—no. Because everybody contribute to it.

Standout Tracks

Westmorelites, "Heighty Tighty" (1968); Keith Porter and Roy Smith, "Cry of a Black Boy" (1971)

- **Bass guitar, vocals**
- **(1953–)**
- **Active from the late 1960s**
- **Member of Westmorelites; Itals**
- **Session musician, session vocalist**

Savanna-la-Mar, Westmoreland, Jamaica, 2005

Clifton Jackson (Jackie Jackson)

More than half of the musicians were not from the city. They were from rural areas, and *deep,* deep into the rural areas also. The great thing about reggae music is that 90 percent of what is being played comes from inside the musicians. Sometime there are musician who can't read, neither notes or chords, but he can play the instrument. And when he takes it up and start to play, it is unbelievable to know that he is not musically trained. Everything, 90 percent of everything, is by *feelings,* you know—*feel.* Yeah. And that's what reggae music is all about. Everything is inside. Inside. Even though the city guys were trained, we were feeling the same thing. They might be a rural musician, but he's feeling the music inside here [pointing to his chest]. And us, the trained one now, when we come together, we forget about our training, you know. We are just playing from inside. So right there and then, we bond together, the country guy and the Kingston guy. We bond. We forget about the training and whatever it is. We forget about the theoretical part of the music. We are just doing the practical part of it, which is what takes over when we are all together.

Standout Tracks

Hopeton Lewis, "Take It Easy" (1966); Paul Simon, "Mother and Child Reunion" (1972)

- **Bass guitar**
- **(1947–)**
- **Active from the mid-1960s**
- **Session musician**

Montego Bay, St. James, Jamaica, 2005

Filberto Callender (Fil)

I need to give credit to Jamaican musicians, who I think were excellent, at the time. During that period [when reggae was being born], I would say, the majority of the musicians were creating. I think that we were hungry to have something that we could attribute to ourselves, as our own art form. Ska was the beginning of it. But to some extent, I think the musicians were tired of some of the North American influences that we were bogged down with. We were forced to play dem, from a dance aspect. If you don't play dis North American hit, you are not popular. We weh had de opportunity to go into de studios, we saw dat as a means to try and create something different. We needed to have something of our own—which we actually didn't have. Because even ska was still a kind of a big band sound, to some extent. So it wasn't all that original, even though it had a little sound [of its own]. So it still needed some more transitioning. And I think that we knew dat. They knew dat, de musicians knew that. And because they have that creativity in them, they were searching, and they were trying different stuff. I think that period was a period of soul searching, to find our own identity, as musicians. And I think we were *very* hungry for it. And we eventually found it. Because rocksteady emerged from ska, and then now, eventually reggae. *Born* was the Jamaican sound now that people could identify with and say, "Yes, this is Jamaican." All of it came together as reggae. Every man is saying, "*I* was the one responsible for reggae, I am the one responsible for reggae." But all of us contributed.

Standout Tracks

On drums: Abyssinians, "Satta Masa Gana" (1969); on guitar: Max Romeo, "Sipple Out Deh (War in a Babylon)" (1975)

- **Drum set, guitar**
- **(1946–)**
- **Active from the mid-1960s**
- **Member of Virtues; Sound Dimension; In Crowd**
- **Session musician**

Kingston, Jamaica, 2005

Larry Marshall

W[ith] every one of my song, I mek my music dem before I mek the song. It come to me inspirationally. The bass line [comes from] my mind. It just come out of me—like it come from *nowhere* to me, and I couldn't refuse it, because those beats was me. When I was a little boy—mek I tell you—my cousin, we used to go to the field where our grandfather and uncle dem work. Sometime we tek water to dem. And sometime we just go dere to help dem do tings, when dem send we for de fire, and go mek up de fire and all these things. We go wid dem. My cousin used to cut this stick—piece of stick like dis, [of a length] about from your shoulder to your fingers—and put it under the arm. [He would] cut two piece of stick now, to play de stick—percussion. Then he cut a [tree] trunk fe me now—a piece of trunk about from there to here—and give it to me fe keep the bass while him playing de [percussion sticks]. So [when] I go to Kingston, when I was recording those songs, *all* those [things] was in me. I said [to the studio musicians], "It need percussion," [or] "It need dis," and whatsoever. They put it, what I want. Because if they didn't do it, I wouldn't record the song. And they want the song.

Standout Tracks

Larry Marshall and Alvin Leslie, "Nanny Goat" (1968); Larry Marshall, "Heavy Heavy Load" (1975)

- **Vocals, songwriter**
- **(1941–)**
- **Active from the early 1960s**
- **Member of Larry and Alvin; Freedom Singers**
- **Lead singer, harmony singer**

Miami, Florida, 2005

Earl Lowe (Little Roy)

I would say music is magic at times. Take a song like "Tribal War." We were in the studio recording. I had a bass player called Lewis. He used to play [rhythm guitar] with Hippy Boys*—Reggie, Alva Lewis. Let I tell you de mystery. We were recording two songs that day. "Tribal War" was playing, and Reggie was playing the bass. And in comes Dennis Brown† to look for us. And Dennis Brown took the bass from Reggie—like he is hearing the song, and he is hearing something. And we make a one-cut riddim—one take—for that song. And that is how "Tribal War" ended up as a hit. Because Dennis Brown, he stepped in, and he was hearing the song, and he was feeling something. So he took the bass same time. And I think that's maybe the only hit song Dennis Brown really played, as a musician. Because that kind of line that he played was more for a learner. But it had vibes. It's not too complicated. It had the vibe. It [was] just right. And then it's just one take. It just played, and it was just so great that we didn't have to make it over. It was so great that [when the drummer] Horsemouth dropped one of his stick—his drumstick—about halfway [through] the song, we still let him play with just one stick.

Standout Tracks

Little Roys, "Bongo Nyah" (1969); Little Roy, "Tribal War" (1974)

- **Vocals, production**
- **(1953–)**
- **Active from the mid-1960s**
- **Lead singer, producer**

*Hippy Boys: group of studio musicians very influential during the period when reggae was emerging. Its members shifted over time, but included keyboardists Lloyd Charmers and Glen Adams, bassist Family Man Barrett, drummer Carlton Barrett, guitarists Alva Lewis and Ronnie Bop, percussionist Tony King, and singer Max Romeo. One version of the group backed some of Bob Marley's most revered recordings (done together with Peter Tosh and Bunny Wailer, as "Bob Marley and the Wailers," and produced by Lee Perry), and two of the members, Family Man and Carlton Barrett, went on to become the rhythm section and creative heart of the band that later achieved worldwide fame as Bob Marley and the Wailers.

†Dennis Emmanuel Brown (1957–1999): probably the most beloved reggae singer among Jamaicans, active from the 1960s through the 1990s. He is often characterized as the "Crown Prince of Reggae," placing him second only to the "King of Reggae," Bob Marley.

London, England, 2010

Lee Perry (Scratch)

Me might not go like regular and work wid de instrument. [But] I have de condition fe play sinting [something]. When they [studio musicians in the early days of reggae] was working, [they were] lucky and never know it. I don't care how much those guy hate me, they could not hate me, because dem love de good [that I did]. De good what me do fe dem, it wasn't money. It was something greater than money, and dem wasn't ready for it. It was a height—a lift, in human magic. And hear what: music is magic. But only some could bless with that touch. Some don't know. No care what dem do, dem won't find it. It's too late. Those [early studio musicians who helped create reggae] was the musician that bless with the touch. So dem can't speak nutten wrong about me. Dem feel it when it happen, and dem see it when it happen. So as dem see it when it happen, it mek dem hear it happen. Then after dem hear it happen, then dem see it, *feel* it happen—and see it happen all till now. That's why some people come inside [the studio at the time] and mek it happen. That's why dem deh.

Standout Tracks

Lee Perry, "People Funny Boy" (1968); Bob Marley and the Wailers, "Duppy Conqueror" (1970)

- **Production, vocals, percussion**
- **(1936–)**
- **Active from the late 1950s**
- **Producer (universally acknowledged as one of Jamaica's most creative producers), lead singer, session vocalist**

Denver, Colorado, 2012

Joseph Hill

Everything begins—even your tone of voice—begins out of love. There is a tone that carry love for the people, and there is another tone that carry no love, because a brother is a brother, and a dollar is a dollar. Some singers sing for the dollar, I sing for my brother. A dollar will come, and the dollar is necessary, but it's not all for the dollar. It [doesn't] significantly rest on the dollar. It rest on my brother.

Standout Tracks

Culture, "Two Sevens Clash" (1977); Culture, "Weeping Eyes" (1979)

- **Vocals, percussion**
- **(1949–2006)**
- **Active from the late 1960s**
- **Member of Soul Defenders; Culture**
- **Lead singer**

Poughkeepsie, New York, 2003

Leroy Wallace (Horsemouth)

I am really for the music from my country—for what I am representative [of]. I appreciate de rest of nation music very much—like American R and B, or whatever they have. We take from each and other. But we were trying to just say the same thing: freedom and social justice. But I like ethnic sounds, and I like de real sounds. I don't like commercial sounds. De real sounds can be commercial, they get commercial after a time, yes, but is very hard, because it's for those who are in de blood. When I'm saying "the blood"—when we say "one blood"—it's deep. It's something that when you're in your mother belly you used to listen to. It sounds like that sometimes. And you just start to play like that, without nobody taught you—without a teacher. You listen, and those songs come out of you, you create your own songs, from no teacher, just from your head, and your mind. So I would say is in de blood.

Standout Tracks

Max Romeo, "Wet Dream" (1968); Burning Spear, "Slavery Days" (1975)

- **Drum set**
- **(1950–)**
- **Active from the mid-1960s**
- **Member of Sound Dimension; Black Disciples**
- **Session musician**

Kitson Town, St. Catherine, Jamaica, 2005

Ansel Collins

Is just inborn in me—the groove, the feelings. Nuff of dem song deh, me mek de intro and all dem ting deh—like "Woman Is Like a Shadow," and a lot of songs. And then me always lead off the pack [in the studio] wid nuff bad word [i.e., curse words] deh—just [for] the *vibes.* You know, [I] give dem de vibe, man, just the feel. You just swear: "Hey! Raas, man! Ready! One, two, three! . . ." Sticky [Thompson] is crazy in dem way deh. Him cuss nuff bad word too [in studio sessions]. Sticky playing percussion, and him have all a bottle, him just break it ina de song and hope dat de song don't spoil—to [give] de vibes, you know. You have fe have it ina you, man. Music must be in you. Music is a inborn ting. When it born ina you, it just stay wid you. Because you have some people weh go a music school and practice it, but dem no have de feel. [Some trained] musician still don't have the feel. Some musician in Jamaica don't love the reggae music. Dem no love it. Dem just feel seh it too simple. Dem a go look a big nation, or why it no reach further. Dem never love it—you know, like how a man will prefer buy de foreign ting deh more dan de local ting. Dem just love the foreign ting dem, the foreign music scene, wid de radio station.

Standout Tracks

Dave Barker and Ansel Collins, "Double Barrel" (1970); Ansel Collins, "Stalag 17" (1974)

- **Piano, organ, vocals**
- **(1949–)**
- **Active from the mid-1960s**
- **Member of Aggrovators; Revolutionaries**
- **Session musician**

Portmore, St. Catherine, Jamaica, 2005

Michael Richards (Mikey Boo)

W[hen] I go to a studio, no one don't really tell me what to play. I [play] from experience and feelings. I'd say this song requires this, or that, and then I complement the song with that. And that's it. Sometimes someone might want a certain thing. They would say, "I really want this." And then you do it. But most of the times—98 percent of the time—it's just what is inside of you that you take out.

Standout Tracks

Peter Tosh, "Maga Dog" (1971); Lorna Bennett, "Breakfast in Bed" (1972)

- **Drum set**
- **(c. 1948–)**
- **Active from the late 1960s**
- **Member of Mighty Diamonds; In Crowd; Now Generation**
- **Session musician**

Kingston, Jamaica, 2005

Peter Austin

We [country people] are already more soulful. We already more easily cry. When people talk to me rough, like Coxsone and all those men, I didn't go around and go on like I was bad, I would stay one side and shed a tear or two. I was very emotional. They used to call me "Cry" [as a nickname]. Not that I am weak. Because I don't want people to take my tears for weakness. But I was very emotional. And so it comes out in your singing—in your voice, in the song. I remember on two occasion, or three occasion, I was recording in de studio, and because of the contents of the song, I started crying whilst I was recording it, and Coxsone have to stop de recording and tell me to go out and cry and come back and finish the song. I'll never forget.

Standout Tracks

Clarendonians, "Rudie Bam Bam" (1966); Clarendonians, "Goodbye Forever" (1967)

- **Vocals**
- **(1944–)**
- **Active from the early 1960s**
- **Member of Clarendonians**
- **Lead singer, session vocalist**

Kingston, Jamaica, 2005

Johnny Moore (Dizzy Johnny)

Music is a wordless language. Music in general is a vibration—emotional transmission. The more emotional the musician is, the sweeter his music. Is just a matter of hearing and feeling. It is able to reach up to the ends of the earth. We [Jamaicans] are special—a special people. Most of the slaves that came to Jamaica are, in a sense, unbroken. So we maintain a lot of that spirituality that came here with us. Even those of us who find ourselves with mixed blood through the raping and the ravishing that went down, we still maintain that connection with the mother country [Africa]. And what we emit [in our music] is the pains of people in general all over the world, because everybody have their problems. And this music is here to alleviate all of that stress, and have you relax and set yourself free.

Standout Tracks

Mellow Cats and Count Ossie, "Rock a Man's Soul" (1961); Skatalites, "Guns of Navarone" (1965)

- **Trumpet**
- **(1938–2008)**
- **Active from the 1950s**
- **Founding member of Skatalites; member of Soul Brothers, Sound Dimension**
- **Session musician**

Kingston, Jamaica, 2005

Keith Anderson (Bob Andy)

The church is a major vehicle for the spiritual consciousness. Church is a major vehicle for the spiritual consciousness and development of slaves and their descendants. [Slaves in America and Jamaica] picked different crops, but it was the same—planting cane or picking apples, planting and picking cotton. Pain is the same to everybody—it hurts. So if you are whipped in Jamaica, you are whipped [in America]. I haven't read any formal history—but I was told that Jamaica was the country chosen for all the slaves [that] were unbearable on other plantations in southern America—[the] South [of the United States]. They would say, "Send them to Jamaica." Our beat is reggae blues. We [Jamaicans] certainly sing blues, but we sing it to a reggae rhythm. They [black Americans] certainly sing blues to a rhythm, but to what they call a blues rhythm. One of the things about Jamaican music: I think if there were a roster of Jamaican music, and there were a hundred [musicians on that roster], 20 percent might have been exposed to some formalized music. So anything else you hear is just *raw* ethnicity—experience as I feel it, or as *she* feels, or as *he* feels it. When you take on Jamaican music, you don't take on a few bars and some melodies, you take on a *culture*—the heartbeat of a people.

Standout Tracks

Bob Andy, "I've Got to Go Back Home" (1967); Bob Andy, "Check It Out" (1974)

- **Vocals, songwriter**
- **(1944–)**
- **Active from the mid-1960s**
- **Member of Paragons**
- **Lead singer, harmony singer, arranger**

Kingston, Jamaica, 2005

Leroy Sibbles (Leroy Heptone)

At first, uptown people] didn't like the [reggae] music. They fought the music. They didn't like it. They didn't like the music. And now it's so strange today—is like all of the uptown youth dem is taking over the business, right now. The sufferers' music, in every country, is always the strongest and best music. Because the sufferer expresses all of these emotions that he goes through daily in his music, man. The musician expresses himself—his hurt, and his pain, and his hunger. The singers, just the same. Because that's our way of *release.* And it's the freedom of release too. It's release without thinking back, or looking back, or looking over your shoulder. It's a natural free and sweet release. So it's no release that you have to apologize about. It's [the] freedom of release. That's what it really is. So, when you let it go, you let it go with all your soul and all your heart. And it comes out like that. It's real. It's natural, it's real. And it's not just Jamaican music. It's music of every depressed people. Anywhere in the world, you'll hear it. You only have to listen to it. Like soul in the U.S., like a lot of African music—any depressed music, you listen [to] it, and if you're a music lover—a person who loves music—[you will hear it]. I don't know how, but you have people who have no time for music. How the *hell?*! They must be deaf!

Standout Tracks

Heptones, "Equal Rights" (1968); on bass guitar: Abyssinians, "Satta Masa Gana" (1969)

- **Vocals, bass guitar, songwriter**
- **(1949–)**
- **Active from the mid-1960s**
- **Member of Heptones, Sound Dimension, Soul Defenders**
- **Lead singer, session musician**

Kingston, Jamaica, 2005

Charles Cameron (Charley Organaire)

Jamaican music], it's always been political. It depends on who is writing [the song]. Because you have the Rastafarians, who are political. You have Marcus Garvey's concepts. You have people who deal with oppression. Because people were being oppressed in Jamaica, and still are. They still are being oppressed. If you notice, most of the artists are from the poor areas—the ones that rise. I think people who have a lot of money, for the most part they're not really concerned about conditions. I mean, there are some. But for the most part, they are not concerned about people suffering. But the sufferers, they're looking at people who are doing great, and then they're looking at people who are doing poorly. It's a rebellious feeling. It comes out with the same thing with love songs—some people rebel against the way they're being treated by that woman, or sometimes it's not them, but they're seeing it happening to somebody else, and they write about it. Because most people write about their experiences, and other people's experiences that they see. So, this is what it is. People are more rebellious in the poorer areas, more so than in the other areas. Let me tell you something about *my* island. It's not racism, but it's a class structure there, where there are people that feel, "You don't measure [up] to me." So, they will treat you a certain way. Because I've experienced that. And that's something I rebelled against. And even in your playing, as an instrumentalist, depending on the nature of the song that you're performing—if that artist is singing a song leading to that idea, then that's what you play, because you feel it. Because you lived it. Because I've lived that type of situation.

Standout Tracks

Maytals, "Sixth and Seventh Books" (1963); Andy and Joey, "You're Wondering Now" (1964)

- **Harmonica, vocals**
- **(1942–)**
- **Active from the late 1950s**
- **Member of Caribbeats**
- **Session musician, lead singer**

Chicago, Illinois, 2003

Leonard Dillon (The Ethiopian, Jack Sparrow)

From we enter de ska [era], it [the music] becomes Jamaicanized. Because we are creating whatsoever you hear. Jamaicans is creating whatsoever you hear. So it becomes Jamaicanized. You are hearing new sounds. And it's created by Jamaicans. De rhythm and blues—we let go that. We are the *sole* responsibility for reggae. *We* create that. Jamaica create that. We are the ones who feel a vibes, and experiment on it.

Standout Tracks

Ethiopians, "Reggae Hit the Town" (1968); Ethiopians, "So You Look Pon It" (1970)

- **Vocals**
- **(1942–2011)**
- **Active from the mid-1960s**
- **Member of Ethiopians**
- **Lead singer, session vocalist**

Port Antonio, Portland, Jamaica, 2005

Wilburn Cole (Stranger Cole)

I don't call it reggae, ska, or rocksteady, or dancehall. I call it Jamaica music. And de mento and all of dem, de whole of dem is like a garden with flowers which glows in different ways—like a garden with many flowers, which give you different colors. I think all music is spiritual. I think it is coming out of a feeling, out of the heart. I think music on a whole is spiritual. I think music is like being a doctor, or a lawyer, or an engineer, a scientist. Music is all about greatness—feeling. The music *is* spiritual. Because, remember, you can hear it—you can't see it. It's like the words coming out of my mouth—I could say anything, but you don't see it, you only hear it. You don't see it, but you hear it. Music—you hear it and feel it. It's *very* spiritual—all over de world.

Standout Tracks

Stranger Cole, "Rough and Tough" (1963); Lester Sterling and Stranger Cole, "Bangarang" (1968)

- **Vocals**
- **(1945–)**
- **Active from the early 1960s**
- **Member of Stranger and Ken; Stranger and Patsy; Stranger and Gladdy**
- **Lead singer**

Kingston, Jamaica, 2008

Nearlin Taitt (Lynn Taitt)

I have a guitar style that they didn't have in Jamaica at that time [when I arrived from Trinidad]. I was there at the right place, at the right time, so to speak. Everybody tell me, "Taitt, you come at the right time, the right country, the right instrument." Jamaica was wide open to me. It was wide open. With music, I'm very lucky. I don't know if luck has anything to do with it, but I'm very lucky. When it's music, no problem there. I think I was there at the right time. I, Roland [Alphonso], Tommy McCook, Jackie [Mittoo], we love music, just love to create music. That was it. We wasn't thinking about fifteen years down the road or so. I tell you that. There's not many musicians who love music the way we loved music. And we loved music beyond anything—beyond woman, man, country, any damn thing. If you understand—we do it [even if we have] no place to live, we'll still [make] music.

Standout Tracks

Hopeton Lewis, "Take It Easy" (1967); Alton Ellis, "Rock Steady" (1967)

- **Guitar**
- **(1934–2010)**
- **Active from the mid-1950s**
- **Member of Dutchy Brothers; Sheiks; Cavaliers; Comets; Jets; Supersonics**
- **Session musician**

Bois Briand, Québec, Canada, 2001

Cecil "Sonny" Bradshaw

The ska era now, those jazz musicians of the period before, that the music changed on, like myself, they could get to play the ska. Because they could now *improvise* as they wish. They were the inventors for that. I've been trying to say that over and over and over again, that the jazz musicians of Jamaica invented the popular music of Jamaica, where it started: the ska. I used to play with them, they used to play with me. Well, after ska, the power [shifted]. I would say the country went into a African period, a period of, "Let's check our roots." And that came out in the drums that Count Ossie* had at Rockfort [in East Kingston]. And almost [all] those progressive musicians, many of them lived in Rockfort. Tommy [McCook] did, Johnny Moore, [and] Don Drummond.† Most of them were in that Rockfort area, where Count Ossie was on his African thing. And they all congregated there. And that's another pocket that started *after,* right after the progressive jazz boys. All these are cycles—the ska cycle, the rocksteady cycle, the reggae cycle. Hey, the reggae music—*that's* the best of Jamaican music, period. Ever. Jamaican reggae music is the best of the Jamaican popular music.

Standout Tracks

Sonny Bradshaw, "Festival Jump Up" (1961); Sonny Bradshaw Seven, "It Must Be" (1970)

- **Trumpet, piano, organ**
- **(1926–2009)**
- **Active from the late 1940s**
- **Member of Eric Deans Orchestra; Sonny Bradshaw Seven**
- **Band leader, arranger**

*Count Ossie: Oswald Williams (1926–1976), Rastafarian drummer who contributed significantly during the 1940s and 1950s to the development of the neotraditional Rastafarian drumming style that came to be known as Nyabinghi. He was one of the most influential figures in introducing Nyabinghi drumming to recording studios and urban popular music, and in the early 1970s he founded (with Cedric "Im" Brooks) the very influential Nyabinghi-based fusion group, Mystic Revelation of Rastafari.

†Tommy McCook (tenor saxophone), Johnny Moore (trumpet), Don Drummond (trombone): founding members of the seminal ska band, the Skatalites. They all started out playing American-style jazz (of the bebop era), as well as rhythm and blues, and made important contributions to the development of ska. Drummond died in 1969, but McCook and Moore continued to work as session musicians and made significant contributions through the rocksteady and reggae eras.

Kingston, Jamaica, 2005

Cedric "Im" Brooks

With the Count Ossie experience, with the Rasta experience, it was limited to just that particular style of drumming, the Rasta drumming, which I could respect. Because that is what they were projecting. And of course Count Ossie was in the mode of evolving this particular kind of music as the identity of Rastafari. As a more general musician, I was aware of all the other cultural elements coming out of Jamaica, which had kept alive the African consciousness. And so the other forms of drumming, like Buru, like Kumina, all those other things—the Revival music—all of those other kind of drumming, were part of the drumming, the African element, that really kept alive the African spirit, even before Rastafari came into existence. And so I wanted to really get some of those music into focus, and really try to utilize the energies coming from those rhythms, and bring it forward to the consciousness of the people again—those things that had kept alive the African traditions over a period of time before Rastafari. So I decided to use as much as I could use within the context of what I was doing. What I saw from Sun Ra* is that he was trying to evolve a new thing from *all* of the stuff that Black peoples in America had. And so he was putting that as a new direction. And so, when I came back [to Jamaica from the United States], I more or less rediscovered the wealth of traditions that we have had here in Jamaica. And not only just the wealth of traditions, but how much they were a *part* of the resistance to the colonial system, and the effort of really maintaining an African identity. So I really thought of bringing it forward.

Standout Tracks

Cedric Brooks and the Invaders, "Ethiopia" (1972); Light of Saba, "Rasta Lead On" (1975)

- **Saxophone, flute, drums**
- **(1943–2013)**
- **Active from the early 1960s**
- **Member of Granville Williams Orchestra; Vagabonds; Mystics; Sound Dimension; Mystic Revelation of Rastafari; Light of Saba; United Africa**
- **Session musician, band leader**

*Sun Ra (born Herman Poole Blount) (1914–1993): visionary North American jazz composer and bandleader. Sun Ra strongly influenced Cedric Brooks after Brooks attended several of his performances and befriended some members of his band while living in the United States during the late 1960s.

Bronx, New York, 2003

Ronald Robinson (Nambo)

In terms of being conscious of the whole development [of Jamaican music], and the creativity, it wasn't something that you really gave much thought. But it was something that you were actually living and experiencing and just growing with, without even consciously saying, "Hey, this is this," or "This is that." It was just a growth for you. For me personally, coming into the thing and actually getting a chance to grow with it, it was like being in a household, and watching, and growing with it. As the initial part, it was mainly a soul-*satisfying* thing for you. And there was a certain pride and feeling of warmth and satisfaction that came from it—your understanding and your knowledge of this music being made by Jamaican people. And sometime you would say, "Hey, this little place—we dependent on everywhere [else] for so long to survive as musicians." Because ina the early part, you'd have people a play swing and blues, and maybe some mambo and cha cha, what have you. But still, there was always mento or bruckins, which was also dance music. They are dance music, coming straight from [the African] motherland. This was a gift that your ancestors gave to you. Actually, this would come back [to you] later, when you sat back and rethink. You'd say, "But, look—this thing [has been going on from] ever since people got here on those ships." This was like a *gift.*

Standout Tracks

Light of Saba, "Rebirth" (1977); Bob Marley and the Wailers, "Wake Up and Live" (1979)

- **Trombone, vocals**
- **(1949–)**
- **Active from the early 1970s**
- **Member of Mystic Revelation of Rastafari; Light of Saba; Ras Brass**
- **Session musician, lead singer**

Kingston, Jamaica, 2005

Eric Donaldson

I never copy a next man voice, his accent. I never try to copy his accent, or to sing or talk like the American. I fall in love with lyrics. Lyrics I really fall in love with. So [American music and song lyrics] only strengthen me to do my work. It only strengthen me to do my work. When you speak Patwa and dem ting, people look down on you as if you're not educated, and you're dark, and ting like dat. [As] I-man see it, it's a form of language, and is a form of way to communicate. And we have to deal wid it. You can't throw it away. Is a Jamaica ting. And this woulda tek you right back to [the] past, to another generation who used to use those things.

Standout Tracks

Eric Donaldson, "Cherry Oh Baby" (1971); Eric Donaldson, "Blue Boot" (1972)

- **Vocals**
- **(1947–)**
- **Active from the mid-1960s**
- **Member of West Indians**
- **Lead singer**

Kent Village, St. Catherine, Jamaica, 2002

Harris Seaton (B. B., Bibby)

You grow up with [the old-time proverbs]. And this is what Bob [Marley] took and conquer the world. Because he's not saying anything that haven't been said before—"foolish dog bark at a flying bird," and all of these sayings. I'm not taking anything from him because he's done that. He was bloody good enough, and clever enough, to do something like that. And it was well done. Sometimes I say to myself, "Why the hell did I change and start to sing in any other way rather than just Patwa?" I should have maintained the thing. Is just that it wasn't accepted. Our parents were saying, "Speak properly! Walk properly! Talk properly!"—that kind of thing. Because we were trying to emulate the English. Because we didn't identify ourself as anything more than just people who want to be either white or upper class or some kind of thing. I saw [eventually] that there was a need to relate to my people. And I think the best way to do it was to do it in Patwa. I used to say to Bob Marley, I used to say, "Bob, why don't you get an interpreter so when you're speaking Patwa people can understand what you're saying?" And he said, "No. If they want to understand, they learn." I say, but he's trying to get the message across. He said, "No, let them learn." And see what happened now?

Standout Tracks

Gaylads, "Africa" (1966); Gaylads, "Joy in the Morning" (1968)

- **Vocals, songwriter, guitar, production**
- **(1944–)**
- **Active from the early 1960s**
- **Member of Winston and Bibby; Gaylads**
- **Lead singer, harmony singer, session musician**

London, England, 2010

Kenneth Farquharson (Ken Parker)

There's a certain *feel* about Jamaica. There's a *feel.* It's like there's some things that cannot be explained in words. But there's a feeling you get that you can't put meaning to. There's a feeling you get. Whether it's a feeling or it's a culture, the type of thing that you get in Jamaica, it's not easily duplicated anywhere else. You see, Jamaica is coming back from what we'd call a rebellious time. You [did] have a rebellion of slavery against those who were in charge [and were] holding a people hostage. After a while, those people who have been held hostage rebel. And it's like a force coming up from the earth—from the ground—rebelling against the established society that was. All that force has not, as it were, disappeared. So all that force is still rising.

Standout Tracks

Ken Parker, "True True True" (1967); Ken Parker, "Only Yesterday" (1969)

- **Vocals**
- **(1943–)**
- **Active from the late 1960s**
- **Member of Blues Blenders**
- **Lead singer**

Fort Lauderdale, Florida, 2005

Dudley Sibley (Duds)

When I used to be at Studio One, Robbie [Bob Marley] used to listen to de foreign artist. When we were dere by ourself, we used to listen. I used to notice him listening to Curtis Mayfield, and all these people. Then, after him listen, him used to seh, "Duds, mek we go down a de back deh." And we used to go *way* around a de back wid some whole heap of bush. And I notice dat when him grab him guitar, him used to play de guitar not like de ska—him strumming like de R and B. But him used to do it his way. Him *turn* it his way. Turn it his way. Robbie was a protest artist, a man who was against the system. And when him started telling me what causing my suffering, I started to adopt his way. And so I realize that I had to do tings my way, even though I [was] influenced by other people. But I had to be me. Robbie used to listen to Curtis Mayfield. We used to listen to all kind of people—Rolling Stones—all kind of people. But Robbie now fit it into a Trench Town experience.

Standout Tracks

Dudley Sibley, "Gun Man" (1966); Dudley Sibley, "Love in Our Nation" (1971)

- **Vocals**
- **(1948–)**
- **Active from the mid-1960s**
- **Lead singer, session vocalist**

Kingston, Jamaica, 2005

Maxwell Smith (Max Romeo)

I think Jamaica is a dynamic country in general. We have our own language, our own music, and our own religion. Moreover, we were the slaves that refused to go to the mainland. We were the unruly ones. We were the bush doctors, and the chiefs from Africa. They left us here, feeling that we wouldn't make it. They wouldn't take us to mainland America. We were the rebels in the pack. And until this day we are known as the rebels in the pack. Jamaicans dem don't take no bullshit from nobody. *Anywhere* we are, we are a force to reckon with. And the world are aware of that. We are the ones who influence the American music now, because rap music comes from deejay music, which is basically Jamaican. We're not just taking from America. We *give* America rap music. We are a rebel. We are rebels with a cause. We're defending our freedom. We want to be free. We are free people. We prefer to *die,* and to go to our grave, than to be a slave. That's our concept.

Standout Tracks

Max Romeo, "Wet Dream" (1968); Max Romeo, "Sipple Out Deh (War in a Babylon)" (1975)

- **Vocals**
- **(1944–)**
- **Active from the mid-1960s**
- **Member of Emotions; Hippy Boys; Upsetters**
- **Lead singer, harmony singer**

Palm, St. Catherine, Jamaica, 2005

Alva Lewis (Reggie)

You see when you come wid de right song? Dat's when de vibes hit you, you know. You going get good riddim. You see when de ting *right?* It *ripe*—just like fruit, me tell you. You see when me a play [in the studio]? Me a look pon de world out deh. Me see de whole world a dance—or de whole world a sing. So me hold imagination. You a imagine, like you ina dreamland. De way how de song sweet me, de word weh you [as a singer] a hit me wid—me a go play it, you know. You see de word weh you a come wid towards me [in the studio]? Me a look pon de world out deh, and seh, "Yes, de world a go enjoy dis." That's how me play.

Standout Tracks

Lester Sterling and Stranger Cole, "Bangarang" (1968); Bob Marley and the Wailers, "My Cup" (1970)

- **Guitar, vocals**
- **(1950–2013)**
- **Active from the late 1960s**
- **Member of Hippy Boys; Upsetters**
- **Session musician, lead singer**

Kingston, Jamaica, 2005

Brent Dowe

I must confess. We weren't looking to the world, we were looking to Jamaica, to create a music of stability, and peace, and harmony, for the people of Jamaica. And we weren't looking for the world to love it that much. It's amazing. [We were] trying to encourage the people, boost them up—[telling them] "All is not lost," and "Something is going on." Because Jamaica is really a tough place to live. Jah know. Music is like the wind. It blows. It blows and it spreads, man, like rain. And I want to spread it some more. I feel [love from the audience]. I feel it inside of me. Sometime I feel this thing from the audience right inside of my chest, like a blow, "boof!"—a nice feeling. I'm very thankful to be able to create such music that people love all over the world.

Standout Tracks

Melodians, "Rivers of Babylon" (1971); Brent Dowe, "Down Here in Babylon" (1975)

- **Vocals**
- **(1946–2006)**
- **Active from the early 1960s**
- **Member of Melodians**
- **Lead singer, harmony singer, session vocalist**

Kingston, Jamaica, 2005

Justin Hinds

It's just coming down from our ancestors—spiritual. When we used to listen to those music, we was in church. So it still exist. My music is the gospel of the Rastaman's music. You'll feel that uplifting from my music, because the music is a project of righteousness to the nation. Because I'm seeing the music as a spiritual force. I will tell the youth dem of the stone that the builder refuse, [how it] become the head cornerstone. And, when you live in a glass house, you must remember not to throw stones. And the higher the monkey climbs [the more he expose]. And you must do all the good to all the people you can, and try to be a straightforward man, because whatsoever you sow you is gonna reap. If you plant corn, you can't reap peas. I will show them within the tradition. My concept within the Rastaman movements is that my music belongs to all race. My belief is that Jah, the Father of the Universe, he was One, and speak the Word. So therefore, if one man speak such word, and became so much people in the world, that means we all are brothers and sisters of the universe. That means that black man blood into me, white man blood into my body, Indian blood into me, Syrian man blood.

Standout Tracks

Justin Hinds and the Dominoes, "Carry Go Bring Come" (1964); Justin Hinds and the Dominoes, "Natty Dread Take Over" (1976)

- **Vocals**
- **(1942–2005)**
- **Active since the early 1960s**
- **Member of Justin Hinds and the Dominoes; Wingless Angels**
- **Lead singer**

Brattleboro, Vermont, 1999

Lloyd Parks

The first musician in the Creation was self-taught. You'd have to be self-taught. When you are self-taught, you will hear a pan knocking [and recognize it as something musical]. Who would think of putting this sound ina music? But I would, because it's a sound. And sometimes you're in the studio, and a man use two bottle [as percussion instruments] and make reggae music. Believe me— I say this with no apology—self-taught musicians are the *greatest* musician. Because when I get together with Sly, it's like magic! He's a great studio musician—Sly Dunbar. I give him credit. Because I know where we started. We used to play on his sister pail, as drum, that [she] wash his clothes in. And I would play the sardine pan guitar dat we make. Because we were youth together, at Waterhouse. And we go under the mango tree in the days, and we play. This is history. Trust me.

Standout Tracks

Ken Boothe, "Everything I Own" (1974); Lloyd Parks, "Officially" (1975)

- **Bass guitar, vocals**
- **(1949–)**
- **Active from the mid-1960s**
- **Member of RHT Invincibles; Termites; Skin, Flesh and Bones; We the People**
- **Lead singer, session musician**

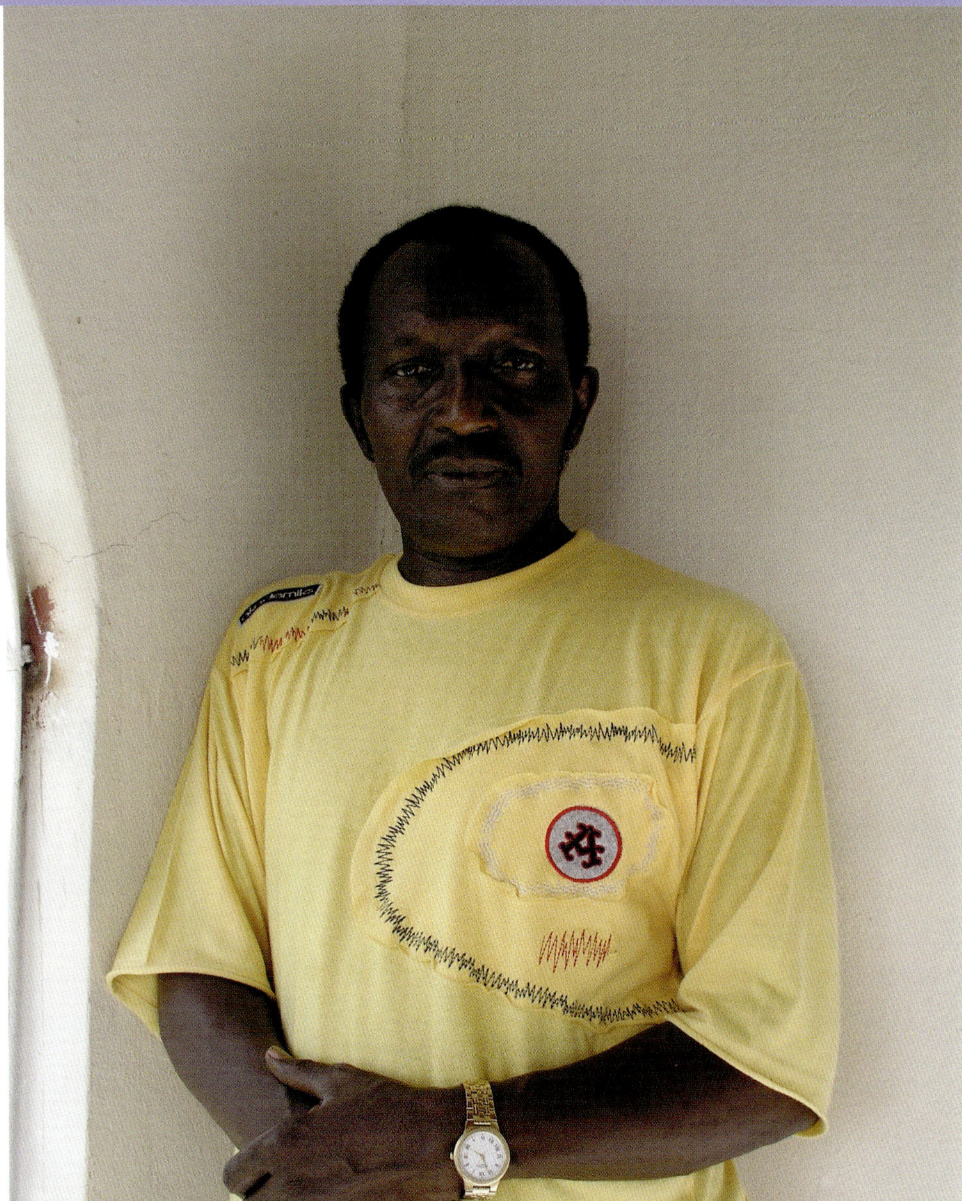

Kingston, Jamaica, 2005

Samuel Scott

In 1951 I made a bamboo sax. And after I made de sax and start to play in de area, dem seh, "All right, you can form a little band." And I get a guitarist, a man named Douglas Freedom, and a banjo man named Solomon Roxborough. And Putun James used to play de drums. I made de drum myself, wid goatskin. I use a round barrel. I cut it, and skin it. And then we mek de drum out of a little keg. And then I tek a spring and made de pedal—de drum pedal weh use wid de foot. And I get a hubcap and mek a cymbal. My band what I have, they used to call it de Scott Band. [That band used to play at] dance and garden parties [around Belmont, Westmoreland]. [My cousin Peter Tosh heard me play] as a young man. And he told me, "Bwai, you going to be a good saxophonist."

- **Saxophone**
- **(1928–)**
- **Active from the early 1950s**
- **Member of The Scott Band; Mighty Queens; Mighty Beeston Mento Band**
- **Occasional session musician**

Beeston Springs, Westmoreland, Jamaica, 2008

Joe Isaacs

Everything comes ina the music from love. And each of us [session musicians] used to love each other, musically. So when we go in, we play together. And there is nothing planned. There's nothing planned, where you say, "Okay, at this point I'm going to do this." No, no, no, no, no. It's just *vibes,* and feelings, that come into these daily creations. And you'd play different little things. Like for a drummer now, I can't go to the studio every day and play the same thing. So I used to have to take different kind of things—like I would find like a bicycle sprocket, I would find like a hubcap. I would find different things to make different sounds. Just like now you have modern technology where they have different electrical devices that can give different sounds. Well, at that point in time now, there was nothing like that. So it was a challenge to me to find different objects that could make different sounds, to create a different impact on these rhythms. Even I take a cowbell, and things like that [that] has been utilized over and over again—some *simple* little things that you would never think of. But those are the little things that created the sound amongst all of us.

Standout Tracks

Bob Marley and the Wailers, "Bend Down Low" (1966); The Cables, "Baby Why" (1968)

- **Drum set**
- **(1949–)**
- **Active from the mid-1960s**
- **Member of Jets; Soul Brothers; Soul Vendors; Sound Dimension**
- **Session musician**

Miami, Florida, 2005

Robert Shakespeare (Robbie)

Jamaican people love music from ever since, you know—quadrille, *all* different type of music. I never used to follow up fe know de name of dem [different styles of music]. But anywhere a little pan knock—"kuk kuk kuk"—I would be there [to listen to the music being made], once it's in walking distance . . . With my playing style and skill now, is a combination of *everything.* Is a combination of everything have a effect with my style. So I can't really pinpoint no individual thing. When it's time to create, I will close my eyes—even on stage, I close my eyes while playing—and I just see it, see the music in front of me. Something come up from five years before—before now. Five years in the future come to me now. It's a God-given talent. And I can't explain it. So if someone ask me to explain it, I can't.

Standout Tracks

Bob Marley and the Wailers, "Concrete Jungle" (1973); Peter Tosh, "African" (1977)

- **Bass guitar, guitar**
- **(1953–)**
- **Active from the early 1970s**
- **Member of Aggrovators; Revolutionaries; Word, Sound and Power; Black Uhuru; Sly and Robbie; Taxi Gang; Compass Point All Stars**

Denver, Colorado, 2013

Winston Riley

Most singers [in Jamaica] come from depressed areas, and music is what keep them together. Music is dem lunch, tea, and dinner. Music will play and let me gather enough food to eat. Music will play, and there is the quickest thing to earn something from, to earn a living from. That's the only alternative quickly you can earn a living from. Say you are down. You're [in] need. And you have a sound [system] come on and start to play. It's free.* An individual will stay dere for de whole night, and will just drink some water, and listen dat, and go to him bed. It mek him happy. It mek him don't feel frustrated. It give him life, give him energy. That's the only thing dat can appeal to him very quick, to make him feel like he's somebody. And peace of mind—that is the main ting. Wid de peace of mind, it give you a feeling to be alive today, and to live tomorrow. And it tell you things that someone can see, and look into what [they] are saying. Some may not, but the majority may see it. And it help you to survive. [When I first started performing, I had to put cardboard in the bottom of my shoes to cover the holes.] Because you can't afford to buy a shoes. But if rain come, you have a problem. Well, you have fe go till you draw a whole heap of rubble ina you foot, until you reach home and catch a bad cold. But that is where I am coming from. That is where most of the guys coming from. Then [the music] uplift him. It inspire him to go further. In the ghetto we had nutten. Nutten was going for dem. You mother and your father can't afford things. And you need the quickest thing to really make a living from.

Standout Tracks

Techniques, "Little Did You Know" (1965); Tenor Saw, "Ring the Alarm" (1985)

- **Vocals, production**
- **(1943–2012)**
- **Active from the early 1960s**
- **Member of Techniques**
- **Lead singer, harmony singer, producer**

*Although most sound system dances, until relatively recently (with the advent of free "street party" dances such as Passa Passa and Weddy Weddy), have charged an entrance fee, the cost of admission generally has been modest. Moreover, the music was loud enough that persons who could not afford to pay could stay just outside the "gates" and still enjoy and move to the sound.

Kingston, Jamaica, 2005

Robert Lyn

Music has no boundaries, as we all know. Being in Jamaica and playing de same type of music, we all have to come together at some spot. You have bands that were formed with certain type of personalities because of where people lived, whether it be up in the hills, the urban areas, midtown, downtown—[the] more roots type of ting, more ganja smoking, as de background for thing. Everybody has to start somewhere. Sometimes it all comes together in the end. Face it—a lot of our performers in general, we are not privileged. They were not well educated. They were not properly schooled in music. And I do know, coming up in de music, that musicians in general—but especially singers who dressed or looked a certain way—were kind of looked down on, and spoken about as "little dutty [dirty] reggae," [or] "nasty Rasta bwai." Bob Marley went through dat. And the fact that you have a little name because you are making records don't really mean that you are anybody in society. And I know that is how they [uptown people] generally felt. It was only *years* after, when Bob Marley started to show how much money was being made by certain people, that some people started [to] take stock, and say, well, maybe these people are worth *something.*

Standout Tracks

Sound Dimension, "Full Up" (1969); Bob Marley and the Wailers, "Black Man Redemption" (1978)

- **Piano, organ**
- **(1951–)**
- **Active from the late 1960s**
- **Member of Sound Dimension; In Crowd; Word, Sound and Power; Revolutionaries**
- **Session musician**

Kingston, Jamaica, 2005

Lowell Dunbar (Sly)

Robbie [Shakespeare] and meself is like a researcher. Because we in a Third World country in Jamaica. And reggae was, to us, young music—I mean, looking at all of that kind of music that's out there. And we always take elements, some other things, and we try to merge it, but still maintain that reggae kind of thing, [so] that you know it's reggae, but you know it's [also] something else. What I try to do, I try to make everything danceable. Because I realize that the culture form of every music is drums. And the drums alone you should be able to dance to, without any other instrumentation around you. So I could be playing [starts drumming on the table, while singing], "healing in de balm-yard." Stanley [Beckford] could be here singing, and I could just playing the drum, and he's singing to just the drumbeat alone, without anybody else around. And you could feel that mento influence, playing just without anybody else. So I learn a whole heap of ting when I seh, well, de drum is really the message in everything, in every form of country—cultural form of the drum. So if you can make that dance, then you could have a congregation of people. I'm not really interested, if it's not danceable.

Standout Tracks

Mighty Diamonds, "Right Time" (1975); Culture, "Innocent Blood" (1978)

- **Drum set, production**
- **(1952–)**
- **Active since early 1970s**
- **Member of RHT Invincibles; Skin, Flesh and Bones; Aggrovators; Revolutionaries; Word, Sound and Power; Black Uhuru; Sly and Robbie; Taxi Gang; Compass Point All Stars**
- **Session musician, producer**

Kingston, Jamaica, 2002

Bobby Ellis

The gardener is the man who plant de ting deh, plant up de place, and mek de place look [beautiful]. And him get de least out of whatsoever remuneration. Well, de same wid we, wid de music business. We [studio musicians] create de whole scenery, and we get de least out of de remuneration. Even de man dat wasn't dere, weh don't business wid it—de disc jockey—get more money than we. Dem get more money than we! We are the gardeners in the business—just a gardener. A we nurture and mek everyting nice. And it's our creation. [But] we don't get no credit [for our] creativity.

Standout Tracks

Bob Andy, "I've Got to Go Back Home" (1967); Burning Spear, "Slavery Days" (1975)

- **Trumpet, flugelhorn**
- **(1932–)**
- **Member of Sound Dimension; Aggrovators; Revolutionaries**
- **Active from the late 1950s**
- **Session musician, horn arranger**

Portmore, St. Catherine, Jamaica, 2005

Ernest Ranglin

As a young fellow, anywhere they have music, I would go there and I would join them. Anything they're playing, I would try to play with them. And I don't try to outplay nobody; I just play with them and enjoy myself, and have fun. You see, I guess that's how the whole thing was organized [in Caribbean music]. [When] you'd play a [European classical] piece—[a] symphony, or something like that—it's the same part you get every time. But with our world, we have ways of improvising, because we leave room-space for the person's imagination. Sometimes we tried to work it out by head [in the studio], because some can't read. So you have to try to find a way of communication. But generally a person who cannot read, they generally have a good ear. And I have an idea of being an ear player before I became a reader. So I think I could communicate with somebody who cannot read. I wouldn't [look down on musicians who couldn't read]. I don't do that. That's why I play with every musician. Any musician out there, I play with *every* one of them. And I never try to throw them off—let's put it that way. Whoever the person is, I play to his ability. And that's the way. Because that's the only way you're going to have fun. When you're going to try to prove [yourself], what are you proving?

Standout Tracks

Wailing Wailers, "It Hurts to Be Alone" (1965); Eric Monty Morris, "Say What You're Saying" (1968)

- **Guitar**
- **(1932–)**
- **Active from the late 1940s**
- **Member of Val Bennett Band; Eric Deans Band; Sound Dimension**
- **Session musician, arranger**

Tower Hill, St. Mary, Jamaica, 2005

Gladstone Anderson

De keyboard is always the leader fe everyting. So after de bass player now listen and find him line, you can seh to him seh, "Give me a rocking feel." Those man have to really *listen.* De whole ting is dat you have fe listen to what de keyboard play. Because him is de one who feel de artist [i.e., the singer]—listen to de artist—and work out de song. You have fe just feel de tempo. You only want de melody now to be sweet. When you get a nice melody to play now, you kind of play around it. Dat is de time de creativeness come in—when you feel de vibes of de singer. From you don't have de feel in you, it not going work. It not going work. It is how you feel it, that's how it come. [Pointing his finger to his heart]: You have to feel it from inside. Dat's really how de riddim creating is. It's by feeling.

Standout Tracks

Don Drummond, "Eastern Standard Time" (1963); Bob Marley and the Wailers, "Bus Dem Shut (Pyaka)" (1968)

- **Piano, organ, vocals**
- **(1934–2015)**
- **Active from the late 1950s**
- **Member of Stranger and Gladdy; Crystalites; Dynamites; Sound Dimension; Aggrovators**
- **Session musician, lead singer**

Kingston, Jamaica, 2008

Tony Chin

Some time, when you go in de studio, you don't know what you gonna play. That's how magical dis ting is. That's how magical it is. We don't know what we're gonna play. Like, we are recording Dennis Brown. Dennis Brown come into de studio, or Gregory Isaacs*. We have not heard de song before. We have not rehearsed wid him. And him go inside and we record a song. Is a feel. So basically that is de first time we hear de song. And it start to arrange. At dat moment de singer is singing de song, we start to arrange ting in our head, going along. And then, after we have a song and dem ting, then we record it on de tape. Well, it might take one, two take, sometime three. But basically it is one or two. De singer didn't compose de music. He compose his lyrics, de song. We just play behind his lyrics. Ninety-eight percent of de time is de musician dem come up wid de music. It was so natural. It was natural to us. Is a challenge, and it's natural. We *enjoy* doing that. It's like we look forward to it. They'd come in one by one, singing. And we just running riddim, all day. We might take a break fe eat lunch or dinner, and then we go back again. So we never hear these songs before in our life, unless is a cover song. Even if that is a cover song, we arrange our feel, put the reggae feel to it. That was basically how de session ting is going. We enjoy that.

Standout Tracks

Bob Marley and the Wailers, "Sun Is Shining" (1970); Niney the Observer, "Blood and Fire" (1971)

- **Guitar, vocals**
- **(1948–)**
- **Active from the late 1960s**
- **Member of Rhythm Raiders; Soul Syndicate; Aggrovators**
- **Session musician**

*Gregory Isaacs (1951–2010): Known as the "Cool Ruler," he was a very popular reggae singer active from the late 1960s until his death in 2010.

Chicago, Illinois, 2007

Val Douglas (Dougie)

A studio musician [is] a different type of musician than a regular musician. Because it has a lot to do with attitude. It's attitude, and being brave. I mean, there are many, many bass lines I have played where I get to a point and I just *do* something, and it's going to be done, regardless of whether nobody like it or not. But I know they're going like it if they really allow themself fe feel it. So it's an attitude, weh you fling someting in somewhere and somebody seh, "*Wow!*!! How you do dat deh?" And then they listen it back and say, "Wow—yeah, yeah!" And then they listen it again and say, "Wow, that wicked!" And de next time they'd be, like, "*Wow!*!!" Each time they hear it, it's so much better. But you have to be able to have that kind of attitude where you *feel* someting. If you feel it going work here, you punch it. You don't be timid and hold back. A lot of musicians are timid. You know?—"Let me do what is the safe thing to do and go through." No. A studio musician—that comes from having enough confidence in what you're doing. Then you can start punching in new stuff.

Standout Tracks

Junior Byles, "Beat Down Babylon" (1971); Lorna Bennett, "Breakfast in Bed" (1972)

- **Bass guitar**
- **(1950–)**
- **Active from the late 1960s**
- **Member of Now Generation; Skatalites; A-Team; Monyaka**
- **Session musician**

Brooklyn, New York, 2010

Michael Chung (Mikey, Mao)

I'm a very spontaneous person. Sometime you do a session and a man deh seh him waan rehearse. Him doing a session next week, but him waan rehearse with a session first. I can't do that. I like to be dere, do the song, hear it fe de first time, [then] ready, let's go. If I play and I know de song already, it's not the same for me. I don't run down anything. When the tape is [rolling], when the red light [is on], whatever I do, it's spontaneous. When you listen it back, sometime you seh, "Whoa—wicked!" But that's how I play.

Standout Tracks

Junior Byles, "Beat Down Babylon" (1971); Peter Tosh, "Bush Doctor" (1978)

- **Guitar, vocals**
- **(1950–)**
- **Active from the late 1960s**
- **Member of Mighty Mystics; Virtues; Now Generation; Word, Sound and Power; Black Uhuru; Compass Point All Stars**
- **Session musician, harmony singer**

Kingston, Jamaica, 2005

Boris Gardiner

I'm a very rough bass player. I can be *mean.* [I can] come up wid some wicked lines. Everybody's in the studio. You listen to a song when a man is singing, and you put yourself in that position, of what the song is saying. And you would kind of live it. You'd play the instrument to how you feel the line should be played. And you'd get ideas as time go by. There's nothing really planned. You don't plan these things. You go on the session, and you listen to the song, and you start humming to yourself, and you start playing what you're feeling on the bass. And it just comes out.

Standout Tracks

Congos, "Row Fisherman" (1977); Boris Gardiner, "I Want to Wake Up with You" (1986)

- **Bass guitar, vocals, songwriter**
- **(1943–)**
- **Active from the early 1960s**
- **Member of Rhythm Aces; Carlos Malcolm and His Afro-Jamaican Rhythms; Boris Gardiner Happening**
- **Lead singer, session musician, band leader**

Kingston, Jamaica, 2005

Larry McDonald

The music will eventually take what it needs to survive. Regardless of the attitudes of the people who playing or the people who listening to it, the music will take what it needs to survive. You can't legislate feel, you see? It's hard to put a finger on it. It's because of the musicians. Nobody talks about Jackie Jackson, [the] bass player. That group of musicians—Jackie, Hux Brown, Winston Wright, Gladdy Anderson, Winston Grennan, and later Paul Douglas—now, that group had a lot to do with setting standards of music—musical standards—stuff that, musically, might be quirky, but it's *totally* correct.

Standout Tracks

Larry McDonald and Denzil Laing, "Name of the Game" (1970); Eric Donaldson, "Cherry Oh Baby" (1971)

- **Drums**
- **(c. 1938–)**
- **Active from the early 1960s**
- **Member of Carlos Malcolm and His Afro-Jamaican Rhythms; Boris Gardiner Happening; Gil Scott-Heron Band**
- **Session musician**

Manhattan, New York, 2005

Joel Brown (Bunny, Noel)

I have worked with musicians—the theory, and practical—and I prefer the musician who does the practical. You know, it's good to read, and good to know how to read it. Everybody should learn how to read music. But the guy that play by just play de music [i.e., reading sheet music] while him watching with them, there's no feel to it. The guy that play with just a feel now, you get more of a feel than the guy who actually read music. Because him [the sight reader] a watch it so much. De people dem who mek music just from reading, you cyaan dance to it. The people weh play out live fe you, you can dance to it. It's the same ting wid engineer. You have some engineers, everyting dem do, dem get de book, and dem read de book, and [say], "It's supposed to sound this way." That's one of the reason why Jamaican music is so very important. That's why it's so good. Because we mix everything in the red [i.e., because Jamaican recording engineers ignore recording conventions about not letting the VU meter needle go into the red zone]. And dem [foreign engineers] no like dat. They couldn't understand it. Now dem start to do it! You know what mek dem do it? The rappers. The rappers is the ones who understand Jamaican music! [In a black American "accent"]: "Listen that bass, man. Damn!" Dem a seh dem waan fe know how come our bass sound like dat and dem own never sound so. So dem seh, "Ah!!" Me seh, pump it in de red! We mix it in the red, bredren! We mix it in the red, and the music come out big and fat!—and nice same way, and more bottom and everything. So you see it go to show you de difference now between a person who deal wid de theory—who read de [notes off] de paper—and then de man weh a *feel.* Feel is what people like. Feel.

Standout Tracks

Noel Brown and the Wildcats, "The Rock Steady" (1966); Bunny Brown and the Chosen Few, "Fat Boy" (1972)

- **Vocals**
- **(1953–)**
- **Active from the early 1960s**
- **Member of Wildcats; Mighty Mystics; Falcons; Chosen Few**
- **Lead singer, harmony singer**

Kingston, Jamaica, 2005

Emmanuel Rodriguez (Rico)

Our music we have fe feel ina we belly. Our music, we have fe feel de punch. So we don't go uptown fe listen to jazz. We waan hear de sound system weh beat we in we belly. For de sound system music is more popular to de Jamaica audience more than jazz. But jazz is something that is accepted in Jamaica, you know. Jamaica have regular jazz sessions every month. [But] a so ghetto people talk, you know. Jamaica ghetto people seh jazz is fe uptown people. Me hear me friend dem seh ina Jamaica, "Rico, me naa go up deh so." And me a tell dem seh I going up a de Pegasus [Hotel] to play. [They say], "Rico, man, a uptown people music dat, man. We naa come, man." Even [when] me tell dem seh I am going to play up dere, they're not coming deh, man. Dem prefer de heavy beat music more. The heavy beat. If dem don't feel it ina dem belly—no.

Standout Tracks

Jiving Juniors, "Over the River" (1961); Rico Rodriguez, "Africa" (1977)

- **Trombone**
- **(1934–2015)**
- **Active from the 1950s**
- **Member of The Rudies; The Specials; Jools Holland's Rhythm and Blues Orchestra**
- **Session musician**

London, England, 2010

Paul Douglas

When we go into the studio to do a song, we don't know how the song is gonna turn out. Some guys do preproduction. Like most of the guys who use drum machine and all that kind of stuff, they do preproduction. That wasn't our thing in the early days. And we still don't like to do that. Because when you go in and you start playing, and this person come up with something else, is nothing that you plan for. It just happen on the spur of the moment, something just happen. And the song just come together all of a sudden, and everything is just gelling. And that's the song. Back in the old days, that is how they used to do sessions—instead of you sit at home and make this thing, and [then] just come in a studio. That's no fun to me. Because you're not thinking anymore.

Standout Tracks

Ken Boothe, "Freedom Street" (1970); Ken Boothe, "Everything I Own" (1974)

- **Drum set**
- **(c. 1950–)**
- **Active from the late 1960s**
- **Member of Beverley's All Stars; Boris Gardiner Happening**
- **Session musician**

Pembroke Pines, Florida, 2005

Dwight Pinkney

The bass line was the foundation [of] a lot of de big songs of that [roots reggae] period. Because the producers used to take so much pride. And even de singers used to take so much pride, and focus so much on coming up wid an *original hard-driving bass line.* A man will come to de studio, and him seh, "Bwai, I *dream* a bass line last night! [It] go like dis." And him start sing, "Tum, tu tun-tu-tum, tu tum." Bwai, de music different nowadays, you know! Because in those days, it really used to *come out* of the people—*come out* of de musicians and the creators. But nowadays, is like factory stuff.

Standout Tracks

Bob Marley and the Wailers, "I'm Gonna Put It On" (1965); Bunny Wailer, "Dance Rock" (1981)

- **Guitar, vocals**
- **(1945–)**
- **Active from the mid-1960s**
- **Member of Sharks; Zap Pow; Roots Radics; Distinguished Personalities**
- **Session musician**

Kingston, Jamaica, 2005

Uzziah Thompson (Sticky)

Me enjoy what me doing in de music. But right now, some tings come in now weh kind of shift certain vibes—dancehall ting. Well, we naa fight against it, because is music same way. But we cyaan fegat de past. And we have fe remember de culture, de roots. For de roots is de roots. You cyaan leave it—de acoustic, de *real* acoustic ina de studio. Well, de computer ting, we don't say no. But de *real* acoustic—de drum, de bass, de guitar, percussion, de keyboard—those are de *real,* real ting. It better when a man sweat and do ting. Him sweat. And when him work done, him sweat, and him do so—[wipes the sweat from his brow]. And you know seh him work from him heart. And dat is de real ting.

Standout Tracks

Skatalites, "Guns of Navarone" (1965); Bob Marley and the Wailers, "Duppy Conqueror" (1970)

- **Percussion, vocals**
- **(1936–2014)**
- **Active from the early 1960s**
- **Member of Revolutionaries; Word, Sound and Power; Compass Point All Stars**
- **Session musician, toaster**

Kingston, Jamaica, 2005

Wycliffe Johnson & Cleveland Browne (Steely and Clevie)

Steely (on the right):

Music at some point always gives me this feeling, the feeling that it can send me a back. The spirit of the music can send you back in time, and teach you something that you never know, without actually knowing [it] physical—like it capture time, like you can go back [into] history, history in general. Is like music, the spirit—the feeling of the mode, and the tone—can take you back, and you can trace history through music. The "Punanny" riddim* was the mother of the dancehall. [It] wasn't about de bass line, really. It was the mento mood of the drum. It was a mento-Pocomania kind of "tun, kéng-ke-teng" [sound]—Revival, that's what we call it. It is the African heritage we have here in Jamaica. Let me explain. We have certain information within ourself that we don't know where it came from. It was handed down by your DNA—information within your heritage, from your foreparents coming down. But what [we] knew then is that in our head we have this feeling to swing ourself a particular way—how to groove ourself. And we wanted a rhythm track that was modern—not really the old Pocomania-mento. Not that flavor, but something of that sort of spirit that will keep us mento dancing. And we worked very hard on dis beat. I seh, "Clevie, let us play the drum this way. Let us do it." Clevie say, "Yes, let us try dis way." And we collaborate together, and create dis ting. When we discover it de day, we jump and say [in a very excited shout], "Whoa-a-a-a-a!!! This is a hit!!" Because we knew then that, yes, we have found it.

- **Steely: Keyboards, production**
- **(1962–2009)**
- **Active from the mid-1970s**
- **Member of Generation Gap; Roots Radics**
- **Session musician, producer**

- **Clevie: Drum set, production**
- **(1959–)**
- **Active from the early 1970s**
- **Member of Browne Bunch; In Crowd; Generation Gap**
- **Session musician, producer**

*"Punanny riddim": the backing track created by Steely and Clevie for Admiral Bailey's 1987 mega-hit, "Punanny," one of the first major digital dancehall hits. ('Punanny' is Jamaican Patwa for "vagina"; Admiral Bailey's hit was in the tradition of earlier sexually explicit songs in the mento genre, such as "Cut Munu" and "Penny Reel.") This backing track, now known as the "Punanny riddim," has been recycled and used as the basis for countless new recordings in Jamaica, and remains popular today.

Kingston, Jamaica, 2005

Clevie (on the left):

I believe dat [Poco] beat probably came wid de slaves. I really think so. And it sounds that way. It feels like it's in your soul. That beat is just in your soul. It was brought here. You see, back then it was a serious thing, in the 1970s going into the '80s. Not just in reggae—all music—musicianship was *key.* You weren't aided by programming, you had to play. You have to have your chops and your licks. I used to practice eight hours a day. I see a generation now of musicians coming up that might be making soulless music for a soulless generation. Because you have those youngsters now that are just materialistic—just *self.* And it's not that the musician who's making that music wouldn't have some success. Because, as I said: soulless music for the soulless generation. I mean, those of us that have been exposed to music with soul and feeling would not gravitate to those songs.

Standout Tracks (Steely)

Bunny Wailer, "Ballroom Floor" (1981); Admiral Bailey, "Punanny" (1987)

Standout Tracks (Clevie)

Sophia George, "Girlie Girlie" (1985); Gregory Peck, "Poco Man Jam" (1990)

Appendix A
Recommended Listening

The following list is limited, with a few exceptions, to compilations of reissued material featuring multiple artists. Virtually all of the most celebrated Jamaican singers, vocal groups, and instrumentalists of the 1960s and 1970s can be heard on the popular music compilations listed here (as well as many who are not as well known but are equally deserving of attention). Such compilations provide a convenient starting point. Just about every one of the studio musicians appearing in this book can be heard on one or another of the releases below, providing the vital musical backing for the vocalists or instrumental soloists, who shine in the spotlight. There is not a single popular music compilation in this list that does not feature some combination of these foundational session players, who most often go uncredited. (Many of the singers or vocal groups represented on these releases with isolated tracks, including lesser-known performers, have also appeared—along with shifting combinations of the same session musicians—on individual albums of their own, and these are certainly worth seeking out as well.) Although some of these albums are out of print, most are still readily available from online retailers in CD format, and some also are available as digital downloads (often with the option of downloading individual tracks). Also included, at the end of this list, is a section featuring relevant documentaries that exist in DVD format (some of which also are available as digital downloads). Because of space limitations, dub compilations (on which the studio musicians featured in this book also can be heard) are not included in this list, although these are worth exploring as well—both for the contributions of these session players and for what such dub versions reveal about the ingenuity and creativity of Jamaica's audio engineers. (For more background on dub music, as well as an extensive list of important dub recordings, see Michael Veal's *Dub Music: Soundscapes and Shattered Songs in Jamaican Reggae,* in Further Reading.) Because the present book is devoted to the earliest generations of Jamaican studio musicians, compilations focusing on Jamaican dancehall music from the mid-1980s on also are omitted here (although a few of the foundational musicians appearing in this book have continued to contribute to popular Jamaican recordings right through the "digital era" and up to the present); but readers are encouraged to explore later forms of Jamaican popular music as well, which continue to display much creative energy and to exert a remarkable influence on the popular music of the world.

All of the following entries, except for those beginning with the name of a particular artist or group, consist of compilations featuring various artists.

Maroon Music

Drums of Defiance: Maroon Music from the Earliest Free Black Communities of Jamaica. (CD) Smithsonian/Folkways. 1992. [1970s–1990s]

Kumina and Poco/Revival

From Kongo to Zion: Three Black Musical Traditions from Jamaica. (LP) Heartbeat. 1983. [1970s]

Jamaica Folk Trance Possession. (2-CD box set) Frémeaux. 2013. [1950s]

Jamaican Ritual Music from the Mountains and Coast. (LP) Lyrichord. 1985. [1970s]

Nyabinghi

Count Ossie and the Mystic Revelation of Rastafari. *The Roots of Reggae: The Original Complete Grounation.* (2-CD box set) Proper/Retro. 1998. [1973]

Count Ossie and the Mystic Revelation of Rastafari. *Tales of Mozambique.* (CD) Dynamic. 1992. [1975]

Ras Michael and the Sons of Negus. *Nyabinghi.* (CD) Creon. 2009. [1974]

Ras Michael and the Sons of Negus. *Rastafari.* (CD) VP. 1991. [1974]

Wingless Angels. *Wingless Angels,* vols. 1 and 2. (2-CD box set) Mindless. 2010. [1990s–2000s]

Churchical Chants of the Nyabingi. (CD) Heartbeat. 1997. [1983]

Trojan Nyahbinghi Box Set. (3-CD box set) Trojan. 2003. [1960s–1970s]

Mento

Stanley Beckford [with the Blue Glaze Mento Band]. *Stanley Beckford Plays Mento.* (CD) Barclay. 2002.

Chin's Calypso Sextet [with Alerth Bedasse]. *Chin's Calypso,* vols. 1–7. (CDs) CD Baby. 2005–2008 [1950s].

Jolly Boys. *Beer Joint and Tailoring.* (CD) Dead Line. 1992.

Jolly Boys. *Great Expectation.* (CD) Entertainment One. 2011. [2009–2010]

Boogu Yagga Gal: Jamaican Mento. (CD) Interstate. 2001. [1950s]

Dip and Fall Back: Classic Jamaican Mento. (2-CD box set) Trojan. 2006. [1950s]

Jamaica-Mento 1951–1958. (2-CD box set) Frémeaux. 2010. [1950s]

Mento Madness: Motta's Jamaican Mento, vol. 2. (CD) 2004. [1951–1956]

Mento Music in Jamaica. (CD) Jamaica Cultural Development Commission. 2000. [1990s]

Soundman Shots: The Caribou and Downbeat 78's Story. (2-CD box set) (second disc features Jamaican and US R and B). Proper. 2009. [1950s]

Take Me to Jamaica: The Story of Jamaican Mento. (CD) Pressure Sounds. 2006. [1950s]

Various Traditional

Cedric "Im" Brooks and the Divine Light. *From Mento to Reggae to Third World Music*. (CD) VP. 2008. [1973]

Bongo, Backra, and Coolie: Jamaican Roots, vols. 1 and 2. (LPs) Folkways. 1975. [1970s]

Ettu, Mento, Revival, Kumina: Recordings from the Jamaica Folk Music Collection. (2-CD box set) Popular African Music. 2006. [1960s–1980s]

From the Grass Roots of Jamaica. (LP) Dynamic. 1970. [1960s]

Jamaican Rhythm and Blues

Jamaica—Rhythm and Blues 1956–1961. (2-CD box set) Frémeaux. 2012. [1950s]

Ska

Skatalites. *Foundation Ska*. (2-CD box set) Heartbeat. 1997. [1960s]

Deep Ska. (4-CD box set) Proper. 2000. [1960s]

Island Presents: Ska. (2-CD box set) Spectrum. 2013. [1960s]

Ska All Mighty: Top Ska Classics from the Treasure Isle Label. (CD) Heartbeat. 2002. [1960s]

Ska Bonanza: The Studio One Ska Years. (2-CD box set) Heartbeat. 1991. [1960s]

Studio One Ska. (CD) Soul Jazz. 2004. [1960s]

Studio One Ska Fever: More Ska Sounds from Sir Coxsone's Downbeat. (CD) Soul Jazz. 2013. [1960s]

The Story of Blue Beat: The Birth of Ska. (3-CD box set) Not Now Music. 2011. [1960s]

Treasure Isle: Ska after Ska after Ska. (CD) Heartbeat. 1998. [1960s]

Trojan Ska Box Set, vols. 1 and 2. (Two 3-CD box sets) Sanctuary. 2000–2004. [1960s]

Rocksteady

Clancy Eccles Presents His Reggae Revue: Rock Steady Intensified! (CD) Heartbeat. 1991. [1960s]

Duke Reid's Treasure Chest: Treasure Isle Rocksteady. (2-CD box set) Heartbeat. 1994. [1960s]

Explosive Rock Steady: Joe Gibbs' Amalgamated Label. (CD) Heartbeat. 1991. [1967–1973]

Island Presents: Rock Steady. (2-CD box set) Spectrum. 2013. [1960s]

Listen to the Music: Caltone's Jamaican 45's. (CD) Pressure Sounds. 2012. [1966–1969]

Mojo Rock Steady. (CD) Heartbeat. 1994. [1960s]

Red Bum Ball: Rare and Unreleased Rocksteady. (CD) Pressure Sounds. 2003. [1966–1968]

Rocksteady: The Roots of Reggae. (CD) Mollselekta. 2009. [2000s]

Safe Travel: The Rare Sounds of Rock Steady. (CD) Pressure Sounds. 2005. [1966–1968]

Studio One Rocksteady. (CD) Soul Jazz. 2014. [1960s]
Trojan Rocksteady Box Set. (3-CD box set) Sanctuary. 2002. [1960s]

Early Reggae

Derrick Harriott: Riding the Musical Chariot. (CD) Heartbeat. 1991. [1960s]
Full Up: Bunny "Striker" Lee's Early Reggae Productions. (CD) Pressure Sounds. 2014. [1960s]
Joe Gibbs: Scorchers from the Early Years. (CD) VP. 2009. [1967–1973]
Joe Gibbs: The Reggae Train. (CD) Trojan. 1994. [1968–1971]
Kingston Town: 18 Reggae Hits. (CD) Heartbeat. 1993. [1960s]
Lloyd Daley's Matador Productions. (CD) Heartbeat. 1995. [1968–1972]
More Hottest Hits from Treasure Isle. (CD) Heartbeat. 1994. [1960s]
Musical Feast: Mrs. Pottinger's High Note and Gayfeet Label. (CD) Heartbeat. 1991. [1960s and 1970s]
The Harder They Come (Deluxe Edition). (2-CD box set). Hip-O. 2003. [1960s and 1970s]

Reggae (some albums also include selections from other stylistic eras)

Lee "Scratch" Perry and Various Artists. *Arkology.* (3-CD box set) Island. 1997. [1970s]
Lee "Scratch" Perry and Various Artists. *I Am the Upsetter.* (4-CD box set) Trojan. 2005. [1960s and 1970s]
Aquarius Rock: The Hip Reggae World of Herman Chin-Loy. (CD) Pressure Sounds. 2004. [1970s]
Best of Studio One, vols. 1 and 2. (CDs) Heartbeat. 1989–1990. [1960s and 1970s]
Channel One Drum Sound: The Revolutionaries. (CD) Pressure Sounds. 2007. [1974–1980]
Hit Bound! The Revolutionary Sound of Channel One. (CD) Heartbeat. 1989. [1970s]
Downbeat the Ruler: Killer Instrumentals from Studio One. (CD) Heartbeat. 2006. [1960s and 1970s]
Feel Like Jumping: The Best of Studio One Women. (CD) Heartbeat. 2000. [1960s and 1970s]
Fire Down Below: Scorchers from Studio One. (CD) Heartbeat. 1995. [1970s]
From the Vaults of Studio One. (CD) Heartbeat. 1991. [1960s and 1970s]
Full Up: Best of Studio One. (CD) Heartbeat. 2006. [1960s and 1970s]
Holy Ground: Alvin Ranglin's G. G. Records. (CD) Heartbeat. 1991. [1960s and 1970s]
Jack Ruby Presents the Black Foundation. (CD) Heartbeat. 2000. [1970s]
Niney the Observer: Observation Station. (CD) Heartbeat. 1991. [1970s]
Reggae Anthology: The Channel One Story. (2-CD box set) VP. 2004. [1970s]
Respect to Studio One. (2-CD box set) Heartbeat. 1994. [1960s–1980s]
Trojan Rastafari Box Set. (3-CD box set) Trojan. 2000. [1970s]

Trojan Roots Box Set. (3-CD box set) Sanctuary. 2002. [1970s]
Trojan Roots Reggae Box Set. (3-CD box set) Trojan. 2005. [1970s]
Roots with Quality: Niney the Observer. (2-CD box set) VP. 2009. [1970s]
Run It Red. (CD) Blood and Fire. 2005. [1970s]
Solid Gold Coxsone Style. (CD) Heartbeat. 1992. [1960s and 1970s]
Studio One Rockers. (CD) Soul Jazz. 2003. [1960s–1980s]
Studio One Roots, vols. 1–3. (CDs) Soul Jazz. 2001–2007. [1960s and 1970s]
Studio One Scorcher: Instrumentals, vols. 1 and 2. (CDs) Soul Jazz. 2002–2006. [1960s and 1970s]
Studio One Women. (CD) Soul Jazz. 2005. [1960s and 1970s]
The Reggae Train: More Great Hits from the High Note Label. (CD) Heartbeat. 2010. [1970s]
Truth and Rights: Observer Style. (CD) Heartbeat. 1994. [1970s]

Historical Overviews (compilations covering multiple eras)

Bob Marley and the Wailers. *Songs of Freedom.* (4-CD box set) Island. 1992. [1960s–1980s]
Bunny Wailer. *Retrospective.* (CD) Shanachie. 1995. [1970s–1990s]
Peter Tosh. *Honorary Citizen.* (3-CD box set) Columbia/Legacy. 2001. [1960s–1980s]
Out of Many: 50 Years of Reggae Music. (3-CD box set) VP. 2012. [1960s–1990s]
Reggae Anthology: Randy's 50th Anniversary. (2-CD/1-DVD box set) VP. 2008. [1960s–1970s]
Reggae Golden Jubilee: Origins of Jamaican Music. (4-CD box set) VP. 2012. [1950s–1990s]
The Reggae Box: The Routes of Jamaican Music. (4-CD box set) Hip-O. 2001. [1960s–1990s]
This Is Reggae Music: The Golden Era. (4-CD box set) Sanctuary. 2004. [1960–1975]
Tougher than Tough: The Story of Jamaican Music. (4-CD box set) Mango. 1993. [1960s–1990s]

Documentaries (films/videos)

Bob Marley. *Marley.* (DVD) Magnolia. 2012. [1960s–1980s]
Lee Scratch Perry. *The Upsetter: The Life and Music of Lee Scratch Perry.* (DVD) Upsetter Films/MVD Visual. 2011. [2000s]
Ernest Ranglin. *Order of Distinction.* (DVD) Aix Entertainment. 2006. [2000s]
Soul Syndicate Band. *Word, Sound and Power.* (DVD) MVD Visual. 2008. [1980]
Dreadlock Rock: The Story of Reggae Music. (DVD) iReality Films. 2012. [1970s–2000s]
Jamaican Music and Soul: Made in Jamaica/The Journey of the Lion. (DVD) Art Manhattan. 2009. [2000s]
Jamdown. (DVD) MVD Visual. 2010. [1980]

Reggae Nashville: Deep Roots Music, vols. 1–3. (DVDs) MVD Visual. 2007–2008. [1982]

RiseUp: Stories from Jamaica's Music Underground. (DVD) RiseUp Entertainment. 2010. [2000s]

Rocksteady: The Roots of Reggae. (DVD) Lightyear Entertainment. 2010. [2000s]

Roots Rock Reggae: Inside the Jamaican Music Scene. (DVD) Shanachie. 2000. [1970s]

Studio One Story. (CD/DVD box set) Soul Jazz. 2002. [1990s and 2000s]

Appendix B
Locations and Dates of Interviews and/or Field Recordings

All interviews conducted, and field recordings made, by Kenneth Bilby, unless otherwise noted.

Glen Adams—Brooklyn, New York, January 24, 2005
Gladstone Anderson—Kingston, Jamaica, February 27, 2008
Keith Anderson (Bob Andy)—Kingston, Jamaica, October 3, 2005
Bobby Aitken—Fort Lauderdale, Florida, October 20, 2005
Herbert Armsby—Spanish Town, St. Catherine, Jamaica, July 14, 1975
Peter Austin—Kingston, Jamaica, May 20, 2005
Neville Baker, Lucille Forbes, and company—Lacovia, St. Elizabeth, Jamaica, January 12, 1991
Stanley Beckford—Riversdale, St. Catherine, Jamaica, January 5, 2002 (interview conducted by Kenneth Bilby and Daniel Neely)
Alerth Bedasse—Kingston, Jamaica, May 25, 2005
Derrick Bell—Old Harbour Bay, St. Catherine, Jamaica, January 30, 2005
Headley Bennett—Kingston, Jamaica, January 25, 2005
Cecil "Sonny" Bradshaw—Kingston, Jamaica, October 15, 2005
Cedric "Im" Brooks—Bronx, New York, October 8, 2003
Joel "Bunny" Brown—Kingston, Jamaica, September 19, 2005
Linford "Hux" Brown—Oakland, California, November 27, 2006
Vira Brown—Coker, St. Elizabeth, Jamaica, February 1, 2004
Cleveland "Clevie" Browne—Kingston, Jamaica, October 15, 2005
Radcliffe "Dougie" Bryan—Portmore, St. Catherine, Jamaica, May 23, 2005
Estavan Callaghan—Hayes, Clarendon, Jamaica, January 23, 2000
Filberto Callender—Kingston, Jamaica, May 16, 2005
Charles Cameron (Charley Organaire)—Chicago, Illinois, November 10, 2003
Cecil Campbell (Prince Buster)—Kingston, Jamaica, October 17, 2005
Tony Chin—Chicago, Illinois, May 9, 2007
Michael Chung—Kingston, Jamaica, October 10, 2005
Claudelle Clarke—Chicago, Illinois, July 9, 2007
Lloyd Clayton (Bro. Job)—Kingston, Jamaica, January 17, 2002
Wilburn "Stranger" Cole—Kingston, Jamaica, March 4, 2008
Ansel Collins—Portmore, St. Catherine, Jamaica, May 29, 2005
Carlton "Santa" Davis—Washington, DC, November 7, 2006

Leonard Dillon—Port Antonio, Portland, Jamaica, January 20, 2005
Eric Donaldson—Kent Village, St. Catherine, Jamaica, January 8, 2002 (interview conducted by Kenneth Bilby and Daniel Neely)
Paul Douglas—Pembroke Pines, Florida, October 22, 2005
Val Douglas—Brooklyn, New York, December 15, 2010
Brent Dowe—Kingston, Jamaica, May 14, 2005
George Dudley—Kingston, Jamaica, May 19, 2005
Lowell "Sly" Dunbar—Kingston, Jamaica, January 14, 2002 (interview conducted by Kenneth Bilby and Daniel Neely)
Bobby Ellis—Portmore, St. Catherine, Jamaica, October 8, 2005
Owen Emmanuel (Count Owen)—Kingston, Jamaica, November 1, 1999
Kenneth Farquharson (Ken Parker)—Fort Lauderdale, Florida, October 19, 2005
Winston Francis—Watford, England, June 1, 2010
George Fulwood—San Clemente, California, November 26, 2006
Freedom Mento Band—Glengoffe, St. Catherine, Jamaica, January 14, 2002
Boris Gardiner—Kingston, Jamaica, October 13, 2005
Owen Gray—Wolverhampton, England, May 26, 2010
Winston Grennan—Bearsville, New York, June 16, 1998
Rafael Griffiths—Braes River, St. Elizabeth, Jamaica, January 8, 2000
Derrick Harriott—Kingston, Jamaica, February 9, 2004
Jerome Haynes (Jah Jerry)—Kingston, Jamaica, May 7, 2005
Michael Henry (Ras Michael)—Los Angeles, California, November 29, 2006
Albert Hewitt (Brother Jack)—Temple Hills, Maryland, December 5, 2005
Joseph Hill—Poughkeepsie, New York, May 29, 2003
Justin Hinds—Brattleboro, Vermont, July 31, 1999
Stanley Hunter (McBeth)—Highgate, St. Mary, Jamaica, May 10, 2005
Joe Isaacs—Telephone interview, August 18, 2013
Clifton "Jackie" Jackson—Montego Bay, St. James, Jamaica, April 29, 2005
Wycliffe "Steely" Johnson—Kingston, Jamaica, October 15, 2005
Kew Park Mento Band—Rat Trap, Westmoreland, Jamaica, January 23, 2002
Kenneth Lara (Lord Laro)—Rose Hall, St. James, Jamaica, January 21, 2002
Alva Lewis—Kingston, Jamaica, May 5, 2005
Earl Lowe (Little Roy)—London, England, May 27, 2010
Robert Lyn—Kingston, Jamaica, May 23, 2005
Eric MacDonald (Brother Joe)—Red Hills, St. Andrew, Jamaica, October 17, 2005
Donald Manning—Miami Gardens, Florida, October 21, 2005
Larry Marshall—Miami, Florida, October 19, 2005
George Matthews—Lionel Town, Clarendon, Jamaica, January 23, 2000
Larry McDonald—Manhattan, New York, December 18, 2005
J. McLaughlin—Lionel Town, Clarendon, Jamaica, January 23, 2000
Bertram "Ranchie" McLean—Kingston, Jamaica, February 26, 2008
Johnny Moore—Kingston, Jamaica, May 21, 2005

Derrick Morgan—Freetown, Clarendon, Jamaica, March 1, 2008
Vincent Morgan—Linstead, St. Catherine, Jamaica, October 4, 2005
Mount Peace Mento Band—Mount Peace, Hanover, Jamaica, April 20, 2005
Cedric Myton—Old Harbour Bay, St. Catherine, Jamaica, January 24, 2005
Emmanuel Palmer—Moore Town, Portland, Jamaica, September 13, 1978
Lammy Palmer—Moore Town, Portland, Jamaica, September 13, 1978
Lloyd Parks—Kingston, Jamaica, May 30, 2005
Alvin "Seeco" Patterson—Kingston, Jamaica, September 18, 2005
Lee "Scratch" Perry—Denver, Colorado, May 26, 2012
Dwight Pinkney—Kingston, Jamaica, October 10, 2005
David Powell—Nain, St. Elizabeth, Jamaica, January 29, 2004
Ernest Ranglin—Tower Hill, St. Mary, Jamaica, September 24, 2005
Evan Lloyd Richards (Richard Ace)—Philadelphia, Pennsylvania, December 6, 2005
Michael Richards (Mikey Boo)—Kingston, Jamaica, May 18, 2005
Edgar Reid—Tredegar Park, St. Catherine, Jamaica, March 9, 1995 (interview conducted by Kenneth Bilby and John Homiak)
Winston Riley—Kingston, Jamaica, October 6, 2005
Allena Robertson—Old Harbour Bay, St. Catherine, Jamaica, January 30, 2005
Arthur Robinson—Kingston, Jamaica, May 18, 2005
Jackie Robinson—Pembroke Pines, Florida, October 21, 2005
Lloyd Robinson—Queens, New York, December 18, 2010
Ronald "Nambo" Robinson—Mannings Hill, St. Andrew, Jamaica, October 12, 2005
Emmanuel "Rico" Rodriguez—London, England, May 7, 2010
Samuel Scott—Belmont, Westmoreland, Jamaica, March 5, 2008
Harris "B. B." Seaton—London, England, May 21, 2010
Robert Shakespeare—Kingston, Jamaica, March 3, 2008
Leroy Sibbles—Kingston, Jamaica, May 31, 2005
Dudley Sibley—Kingston, Jamaica, January 26, 2005
Noel "Skully" Simms—Kingston, Jamaica, October 9, 2005
Maxwell Smith (Max Romeo)—Palm, St. Catherine, Jamaica, October 2, 2005
Roy "Spar" Smith—Savanna-la-Mar, Westmoreland, Jamaica, May 12, 2005
Nearlin "Lynn" Taitt—Bois Briand, Québec, Canada—August 30, 2001 (interview conducted by Kenneth Bilby and Jim Dooley)
Uzziah "Sticky" Thompson—Kingston, Jamaica, May 30, 2005
Leroy "Horsemouth" Wallace—Kitson Town, St. Catherine, Jamaica, May 15, 2005
Ivanhoe Wilson—Richmond, St. Mary, Jamaica, January 10, 2005
Rev. Otis Wright—Elmont, New York, December 18, 2010

Glossary

Babylon
Rastafarian term denoting the oppressive structures of Western society, the police, and the forces of evil more generally.

Binghi See Nyabinghi

bruckins
Type of dance and music associated with emancipation celebrations in the eastern part of Jamaica.

Buru (also sometimes spelled Burru)
African-Jamaican music and dance tradition associated with the Christmas season, originally involving masking, veneration of ancestors, and sung criticism. When people from rural areas brought Buru music to West Kingston in the 1940s and 1950s, early Rastafarians living in the same areas adopted the three drums of Buru—the *repeater, funde,* and *bass*—and drawing on various sources (including Buru music), created their own new music that became known as *Nyabinghi.* Older, non-Rastafarian forms of Buru continue to be practiced in some areas today and remain musically distinct from Nyabinghi.

deejay (or DJ)
In Jamaica, this refers specifically to a performer who rhythmically speaks or intones (rather than sings) lyrics over a musical backing track (similar to a rapper or MC/emcee in the US hip-hop tradition). *Deejaying* (or *toasting,* as it was known at first) developed in Jamaica as a major offshoot of the reggae tradition during the 1970s, and became dominant during the 1980s and 1990s. It remains the leading form of vocal expression in contemporary Jamaican dancehall music.

digital music
In Jamaican popular music, the term "digital" is sometimes used (interchangeably with "computerized") to refer to any music that makes prominent use of programmable instruments (such as drum machines), not just music recorded in digital formats and manipulated with software such as Pro Tools. Most of what is thought of as the digital (or computerized) dancehall music of the 1980s and 1990s, though it relied heavily on synthesized sounds and programmable instruments, was actually recorded using analog technology and production techniques. Only after 2000 did Jamaican studios begin to rely on fully digital recording technology.

duppy
Spirit of a deceased human being; ghost.

gere (sometimes spelled gerre, or gerreh)
Type of African-influenced wake music found in western parishes of Jamaica.

gospel (Jamaican gospel)

A distinct variety of Protestant gospel music that developed in Jamaica during the 1960s and 1970s in tandem with reggae, blending elements of African-American gospel and American country (including "white" gospel) music with local Revival music, mento, reggae, and other indigenous Jamaican influences. Otis Wright (who appears in this book) is often thought of as the "father of Jamaican gospel." Claudelle Clarke (also in this book) was another prominent early proponent.

gumbe

Type of rectangular frame drum used in the African-Jamaican religious tradition known as *Gumbe Play.* The gumbe is found primarily in the western parishes of Manchester and St. Elizabeth (including the Maroon community of Accompong), but is also used in some Maroon communities in the eastern part of the island. It is also associated with older variants of *Jonkonnu* in a few communities.

Jonkonnu (or Jankunu)

African-Jamaican festival tradition associated with the Christmas holidays, usually involving masking, drumming, dancing, and parading. The tradition developed during the slavery era, possibly as early as the late seventeenth century. It originally used the *gumbe* drum and featured a large headdress in the form of a house (itself called the *Jankunu*). Over time it merged with European-influenced masquerade traditions and today is most often backed by the music of fife-and-drum ensembles that show both African and European influence.

Kumina

African-Jamaican religion introduced to the island by indentured African laborers who arrived after the abolition of slavery in 1834. Derived largely from Central African (especially Kongo) sources, it is found primarily in the eastern part of the island, and is identified particularly strongly with St. Thomas parish. Its music, also known as Kumina, is based on an ensemble of two drums, the *bandu* (or *kibandu*) and *kyas,* which provide the rhythms for sacred dance and are used to invoke the spirits of African ancestors. Kumina music also was adopted by the earliest Rastafarians in the 1930s, under the leadership of prophet Leonard Howell, and was used for worship in the commune he founded at Pinnacle in 1940, but later was supplanted among most Rastafari worshippers by Nyabinghi music and drumming.

mento

Indigenous Jamaican style of music, dance, and song developed during the nineteenth century from both African and European sources. It often is compared to Trinidad's calypso, which influenced it during the twentieth century, but it has remained distinct. Most often played by string bands featuring four-string banjo, guitar, rumba box (bass lamellophone), and a variety of percussion instruments, it also can incorporate fife, violin, either bamboo or factory-made saxophone, harmonica, and any number of other instruments. Before ska emerged in the early 1960s, mento was the closest thing to a national popular music, and a limited number of commercial mento recordings were made in Kingston and released on fledgling local labels during the 1950s.

myal

Jamaican term referring to the state of being possessed by a spirit (most often an ancestor). The term usually has positive connotations, most often referring to spirits that are purposefully invoked through music and dance for healing or other kinds of help. Today it is limited mostly to the older, more African religious traditions that continue to be practiced in certain parts of the island, such as Kumina, or the Maroon Kromanti religion.

nine night (also known as Dead Yard)

African-Jamaican ceremony traditionally held nine days after death to honor a deceased person, appease his or her spirit, and aid its transition to the afterlife. A nine night typically consists of an all-night wake (*setup*) during which food and drinks are served and traditional hymns are performed, sometimes alongside other kinds of traditional music and dance such as mento, gere, dinki mini, or Kumina. A recent innovation is the "duppy band" (spirit band), a kind of semi-professional ensemble specializing in nine night performances, often featuring a drum kit (traps) and some combination of electric and/or traditional instruments.

Nyabinghi (also known as Binghi)

Rastafarian ceremony of worship and associated music and dance. Nyabinghi music, based on an ensemble of three drums—the *repeater* (sometimes called *kete*), the *funde,* and the *bass*—grew out of the earlier *Buru* drumming tradition, which was adopted and modified by Rastafarians living in West Kingston during the 1950s, and also was influenced by *Kumina* drumming.

Patwa (from "patois")

The name used by Jamaicans to refer to the African-influenced creole language of Jamaica, which is considered by some linguists to be a distinct language, separate from (though related to) English. Although English is the official language of the country, Patwa is the most widely spoken language.

Pocomania (often abbreviated as Poco)

Term commonly used to refer to any of the more African-identified forms of Jamaican Revivalism (see *Revival*). The etymology of Pocomania is unknown (although the term may be of African derivation). There is no evidence that its origins have anything to do with Spanish *poco* ("little") or English *mania,* as a common folk etymology would have it. To avoid the negative associations of this folk etymology (which could lead to the conclusion that the term originally meant "little madness"), some urban intellectuals have adopted the spelling *Pukkumina,* to suggest that the term is derived partly from *Kumina.* But neither the history of Jamaican Revivalism nor the most common "folk" pronunciations of the term (/pókomínya/ or /pókoméinya/) support this derivation. Most Jamaicans continue to pronounce the term in the older way and, when writing it, most often render it as *Pocomania.*

quadrille

Indigenized Jamaican version of the European dance of the same name, consisting of various "figures" (and, in Jamaica, incorporating indigenized versions of a number of related nineteenth-century ballroom dances as well). Usually performed by string bands, local versions of quadrille music played an important role in the emergence of mento during the nineteenth century. Quadrille continues to form part of the repertoire of some rural mento bands today.

Revival

Blanket term covering all varieties of Jamaica's indigenous Afro-Protestant religion, which emerged during the slavery era in response to missionization. The earliest practitioners referred to themselves as Native Baptists, and they blended Christian and African concepts to produce a distinctively African-Jamaican form of worship. The terms *Revival* and *Pocomania* are often used interchangeably, although some practitioners claim distinctions between the two, typically attributing a more African character to the latter. There are hundreds of Revival churches spread across the island, in both rural and urban areas, and imported varieties of Protestantism such as Pentecostalism have to some extent been indigenized through absorption of elements from Revival. Revival has a vibrant musical tradition that blends traditional Protestant hymns and indigenous Jamaican spiritual songs with body percussion (such as clapping and stamping), loud rhythmic breathing (known as trumping, groaning, or laboring), and sometimes vigorous drumming. The music and dance often lead to spirit possession and/or trance. Revival music and other aspects of the tradition continue to exert a powerful influence in Jamaican society.

sound systems (sometimes referred to simply as sounds)

High-powered mobile audio playback systems (originally consisting of a turntable, amplifier, and large homemade speaker boxes) that began to provide music for outdoor dances in Kingston and other parts of the island in the late 1940s. In the 1950s and the following decades, sound systems proliferated and grew in size, playing records at increasingly high volume and attracting large crowds. Rival sound systems (bearing colorful names) began to compete for supporters, and over time the tradition of the "sound clash" developed, pitting two or more sounds in musical battles to determine which had the greatest (and rarest) records and most skillful record selectors (winners being determined by crowd responses). Sound systems quickly evolved into the single most important means for people in poorer neighborhoods to hear, enjoy, and dance to local recorded music, and became crucial to the process of making local and national hits. They also were closely associated with the development of toasting or deejaying as a distinctive verbal art form, and became a primary venue for live performances by deejays. Sound systems remain a fundamentally important part of Jamaican popular music, and Jamaican-style sound systems have spread to many other countries. Now Jamaican sets often travel to other parts of the world for international clashes with foreign sound systems.

Further Reading

Literature based on substantial interviews with Jamaican singers and/or musicians, or other firsthand accounts.

Augustyn, Heather. *Don Drummond.* Jefferson, NC: McFarland, 2013.

———. *Ska: An Oral History.* Jefferson, NC: McFarland, 2010.

———. *Songbirds: Pioneering Women in Jamaican Music.* Chesterton, IN: Half Pint Press, 2014.

Barrow, Steve, and Peter Dalton, eds. *The Rough Guide to Reggae.* 3rd ed. London: Rough Guides, 2004.

Bilby, Kenneth. "Distant Drums: The Unsung Contribution of African-Jamaican Percussion to Popular Music at Home and Abroad." *Caribbean Quarterly* 56, no. 4 (2010): 1–21.

———. "Jamaica." In Peter Manuel, Kenneth Bilby, and Michael Largey, *Caribbean Currents: Caribbean Music from Rumba to Reggae,* 143–82. Philadelphia: Temple University Press, 1995.

Bilby, Kenneth, and Elliott Leib. "Kumina, the Howellite Church and the Emergence of Rastafarian Traditional Music in Jamaica." *Jamaica Journal* 19, no. 3 (1985): 22–28.

Bilby, Kenneth, and Fu-Kiau kia Bunseki. *Kumina: A Kongo-Based Tradition in the New World.* Brussels: Centre d'Étude et de Documentation Africaines, 1983.

Bradley, Lloyd. *This Is Reggae Music: The Story of Jamaica's Music.* New York: Grove Press, 2000.

C, Gordon. *The Reggae Files.* London: Hansib, 1988.

Coester, Markus, and Wolfgang Benders, eds. *A Reader in African-Jamaican Music, Dance and Religion.* Kingston, JM: Ian Randle Publishers, 2015

Davis, Stephen, and Peter Simon. *Reggae Bloodlines: In Search of the Music and Culture of Jamaica.* Garden City, NY: Anchor Press, 1977.

———. *Reggae International.* New York: R and B, 1982.

Foster, Chuck. *Roots, Rock, Reggae: An Oral History of Reggae Music from Ska to Dancehall.* New York: Billboard, 1999.

Hawks, Noel, and Jah Floyd. *Reggae Going International 1967–1976: The Bunny "Striker" Lee Story.* London: Jamaican Recordings, 2012.

Hitchins, Ray. *Vibe Merchants: The Sound Creators of Jamaican Popular Music.* Burlington, VT: Ashgate, 2014.

Jahn, Brian, and Tom Weber. *Reggae Island: Jamaican Music in the Digital Age.* New York: Da Capo Press, 1998.

Johnson, Howard, and Jim Pines. *Reggae: Deep Roots Music.* London: Proteus, 1982.

Kaski, Tero, ed. *More Axe: Mud Cannot Settle without Water*. Kuusankoski, FI: Black Star, 1998.

Katz, David. *People Funny Boy: The Genius of Lee "Scratch" Perry*. London: Omnibus Press, 2006.

———. *Solid Foundation: An Oral History of Reggae*. Rev. and exp. ed. London: Jawbone Press, 2012.

Kroubo Dagnini, Jérémie. *Vibrations jamaïcaines: L'Histoire des musiques populaires jamaïcaines au XXe siècle*. Rosières en Haye, FR: Camion Blanc, 2011.

Lesser, Beth. *Dancehall: The Rise of Jamaican Dancehall Culture*. London: Soul Jazz, 2008.

———. *Rub-a-Dub Style: The Roots of Modern Dancehall*. Toronto: Beth Kingston, 2012.

Lewin, Olive. *Rock It Come Over: The Folk Music of Jamaica*. Kingston, JM: University of the West Indies Press, 2000.

Masouri, John. *The Life of Peter Tosh: Steppin' Razor*. London: Omnibus, 2013.

———. *The Story of Bob Marley's Wailers: Wailing Blues*. London: Omnibus, 2008.

Neely, Daniel T. "Mento, Jamaica's Original Music." PhD diss., New York University, 2008.

Steffens, Roger. *So Much Things to Say: The Oral History of Bob Marley*. New York: W. W. Norton, 2016.

Steffens, Roger, and Leroy Jodie Pierson. *Bob Marley and the Wailers: The Definitive Discography*. Cambridge, MA: Rounder Books, 2005.

Stolzoff, Norman C. *Wake the Town and Tell the People: Dancehall Culture in Jamaica*. Durham, NC: Duke University Press, 2000.

Veal, Michael E. *Dub: Soundscapes and Shattered Songs in Jamaican Reggae*. Middletown, CT: Wesleyan University Press, 2007.

Whitney, Malika Lee, and Dermot Hussey. *Bob Marley: Reggae King of the World*. New York: E. P. Dutton, 1984.

Index

Page numbers in italics refer to featured interview texts and/or photographs.

Music:Interview

A SERIES FROM WESLEYAN UNIVERSITY PRESS

Edited by Daniel Cavicchi

The Music/Interview series features conversations with musicians, producers, and other significant figures in the world of music, past and present. The focus is on people who have not only made good music but have had insightful and profound things to say about creativity, politics, and culture. Each Music/Interview book presents an original approach to music-making, showing music as a vehicle for inspiration, identity, comment, and engagement. The interview format provides conversations between knowledgeable insiders. By foregrounding individual voices, the series gives readers the opportunity to better appreciate the sounds and music around us, through the voices of those who have experienced music most directly.

Yip Harburg
Legendary Lyricist and Human Rights Activist
Harriet Hyman Alonso

Fela
Kalakuta Notes
John Collins

Words of Our Mouth, Meditations of Our Heart
Pioneering Musicians of Ska, Rocksteady, Reggae, and Dancehall
Kenneth Bilby

Reel History
The Lost Archive of Juma Sultan and the Aboriginal Music Society
Stephen Farina

Producing Country
The Inside Story of the Great Recordings
Michael Jarrett

Always in Trouble
An Oral History of ESP-Disk', the Most Outrageous Record Label in America
Jason Weiss

About the Author

Kenneth Bilby is an ethnomusicologist, writer, and expert on Jamaican and other Caribbean music. He is the former director of research at the Center for Black Music Research at Columbia College Chicago and currently a research associate at the Smithsonian Institution. He has taught at Bard College, Regis University, and the University of Colorado at Boulder. He is the author of *True-Born Maroons* and co-author of *Caribbean Currents: Caribbean Music from Rumba to Reggae*. His field recordings of Jamaican traditional music represent arguably the largest such collection in the world.